A GUIDE TO
PERSONAL
RISK
TAKING

A GUIDE TO PERSONAL RISK TAKING

RICHARD E. BYRD

amacom

A Division of American Management Associations

Library of Congress Cataloging in Publication Data

Byrd, Richard F
    A guide to personal risk taking.

    Bibliography
        1.   Risk.   2.   Middle managers.   I.   Title.
HD61.B95   658.4'3   74-75169
ISBN 0-8144-5363-5
ISBN 0-8144-7505-1 pbk

First AMACOM paperback edition 1978.

To those who bet on me:

HENRY LEE
RUSS
RUXTON
REYNOLDS
DAN
ELSA
M. ROBERT

Preface

THIS BOOK is about risk-taking behavior, especially as it applies to middle managers. My purpose is to stir the middle managers of industry, business, government, church, and voluntary agencies to take more short-run chances for long-run gains.

Gamblers have a phrase for risk taking: betting on the come. To the crapshooter, betting on the come is the promise of a new number, of a new game, with new odds. To the businessman, it is taking action that is based on the expected result of a future event. Middle managers never really have cultivated this sport. The kinds of risks they characteristically take lead to long-run gains that are more like the promise of a plot in a cemetery than a reward whose benefits they can enjoy. But then, middle managers have their own special characteristics.

I've spent a long time puzzling over just who middle managers are. Even at a recent AMA conference, no one could produce a totally acceptable definition because titles and responsibilities differ so greatly across organizations. The conference arbitrarily called those people with "manager" in their title middle managers. Another definition could be everyone above foreman.

After much consideration, I believe that middle manager, like middle class, is a state of mind rather than simply a particular type of supervisory position. All middle managers tend to be scared of the same things and to be in the nexus of the same organizational forces. They tend to want the same kinds of bene-fits. They are alike in what they will and won't risk, and they tend to be angry and frustrated by the same constrictions or bureau-cratic conditions. This is true in manufacturing concerns, church hierarchies, engineering firms, federal and city bureaucracies, school systems, university faculties, volunteer organizations, the military, and so forth. Some of this mentality is inherent in certain executive positions. It even exists in some first-line supervisors. Mainly, however, it is the property of the great majority between the executive and the first-line supervisor.

All is not amiss! The middle class of management has much to offer. It runs most of the world, even now. There is, however, room for improvement, and I will outline the steps by which those who want to expand their capacities and want to contribute more can reach their goals. In the first section of the book I tell the truth as I see it, in as straight a way as possible, using research and experience to understand the middle manager's plight. Then, in the second half, I offer help in a very prescriptive "Have you tried this?" manner.

Many teachers, friends, colleagues, and clients, too numerous to mention, have contributed to the ideas in this book. Frank Howard and Robert Metcalf gave me the definitions of betting on the come used throughout the book. My colleagues also helped. John Cowan critically reviewed the text. Polly Mead helped on the planning concepts. Those having the greatest impact have been my wife and reality tester, Helen; my editors, Barbara Neilson and Mary Louise Byrd; my secretary, Ann La Bissonniere, who typed the slush I handed her; and my daughter, Jackie, who edited out much of my sexism. But for them, this book would not be in your hands.

Richard E. Byrd

Contents

UNIT FOUR
ORGANIZATIONAL RISK MANAGEMENT

APPENDIXES

A GUIDE TO
PERSONAL
RISK
TAKING

Introduction

THIS BOOK is polemic, not scientific, in style. No pretense is made to present balanced views. I am only talking to the middle managers about themselves. Whatever the reader's orientation, let me say that the contents of this book are neither to be taken as a program for how to make middle managers work harder nor as a proposal for organizing a threat to top management. I hope this book will be the mirror that shows the moderately discontented, disenchanted, and often alienated middle managers that it is their job to fulfill their needs. They can either do this within their present vocation and organization or change one or both. But fulfill themselves they must, for everyone's benefit — their family's, top management's, and their community's. The very health and productivity of our nation may depend upon it in the next competitive decade.

An HEW report, *Work in America*,[1] reflected that meaningful work, adequate working conditions, proper equipment, and responsibility were considered more important than compensation beyond certain maintenance needs for American workers in general. *Manager Unions?*, a 1972 AMA Research Report, examined the responses of approximately 3,000 people in business whose title included the word "manager." Without question, their frustrations were not primarily money motivated. Managers of today report that

1

... opportunities for direct participation in the decision-making process seem to be rapidly decreasing in the highly bureaucratic and authoritarian structure of the technocorporation of the 1970s.

Many managers report a decreasing sense of excitement in managing. Where, they ask, is the challenge, adventure, motivation, competitive spirit, sense of personal fulfillment, creativity, drive, purpose, ingenuity once required of managers in the pursuit of corporate growth and individual excellence? One manager, commenting for this report, considers even his title a misnomer. "You have misaddressed the envelope containing this questionnaire," he wrote. "I am not the 'Purchasing Manager.' I am the chief functionary of the purchasing function." [2]

The report doesn't delve into the specific frustrations of minority and women managers. Their problems are above and beyond those of nonminority managers. In the federal government, as in industry, the proportion of women workers is increasing, but the number of women managers is proportionately decreasing. While the number of minority managers are gradually increasing, the hopes of minority managers generally serving in top management had best be forgotten if the present trend continues.

The AMA report hints loudly that executive management had better "do something" about this crisis situation. "Executive management will put itself in great peril if it neglects to recognize fully the changing spirit of the times and the changing values and new life-styles which are appearing especially, but not exclusively, among the younger generation of managers." The specter of management unionizing hovers threateningly if top management doesn't respond. For example, there are already many professional and managerial associations — even unions — for school principals, airline pilots, and clergy. These associations seem to emerge when executive management will not consider the grievances of these employees as individuals.

The fact remains that pointing out the union threat and emphasizing the unions already formed will not convince executive management of the need to act in newly benevolent, patriarchal ways. In point of fact, such behavior on its part should be viewed as unhealthy paternalism. However, executive management tends to do nothing at all. It seems to prefer to keep its eye on the market, on corporate trends, on potential mergers, tax problems, long-range planning, and improvement of capital positions. One might argue that top managements should also be concerned for the development of their middle managers as well as the rest of their human resources. Some are, some try to, and still others pretend to. But the major task of executive management will remain external, not internal. For that reason, little energy can be expected to solve middle manager problems until an actual crisis threatens.

This book, then, is not about what executive management should do to relieve the boredom and inhumanity of organizational life for the middle manager. Executives reading this book would not deny, perhaps for themselves as well as for middle management, the need for such relief. However, no one can create the kind of motivation the middle manager needs—except the middle managers themselves. Senior management is often admonished to motivate middle managers, but no one can give another person "challenge, adventure, motivation, a competitive spirit, a sense of personal fulfillment, drive, purpose, and ingenuity." Each individual either demands a working environment that permits those motivations to be realized or takes the risk to go elsewhere.

For practical reasons, if not for any other reason, this book must assume that the major enemies of middle managers are the middle managers themselves. If they seek personal realization and take the risks necessary to achieve it, then, depending on the particular bureaucracy they live in, chances are there will be rewards and punishment aplenty. Sadly, middle managers have learned to sell their freedom for regular hours, no layoffs, wearing a suit, broken promises, profit-sharing and/or pension plans with lengthy investiture periods—and, based on that security, staggering personal debt loads. The chains are real. They know. They put them on themselves.

If you are a middle manager you might well reply that executive management is to blame because it enticed you into your present situation. You may ask, "What happened to the promises executive management made during the sixties? Were they lying to us about the unlimited opportunities of the future? We look around now and see lateral advancement, at best, as a possibility in these slower economic growth periods." My response is that no person, company, or government should make the apparently unrequited promise of advancement and security often made by top management to an eagerly accepting audience of new employees who want to believe they will soon be president. L. C. Wynn et al. describe the same phenomenon as occurring within a schizophrenic family.[3] In the schizophrenic family there is a kind of pseudomutuality such as occurred between executive and middle management, where one said what the other wanted to hear. Both wanted to be duped. Both were.

Take a look at the facts. Was, then, the promised security a basis for challenge, adventure, motivation, competitive spirit, and so on? Of course, executive management promised a rosy future. The answer is yes, it lied, in the sense that the young lover promises his love everything when, in reality, very little is possible. Yes, you wanted to believe it, so you colluded in the proposition.

A good description of middle management's dilemma is that of Michael R. Barrett, assistant editor of *Plant Management & Engineering*. He says

> The middle management executive is the carnival juggler in the center ring of the corporate circus. He must balance top management productivity requests against the capabilities of laborers; he must perform tasks that require much skill, but have few rewards. No one remembers the juggler if he is successful, but have him drop something and watch the heads turn.[4]

Such a dilemma may lead to systematic low risk, which endangers the future of organizations and the mental health of some very nice people.

In summary, this book declares to you, the middle manager, that your condition is first of all a product of your own creation, originally based on your blind ambition. No matter what part executive management played or plays in your present dilemma, your situation is your problem and your responsibility to solve. Do something! This book is designed to give you a variety of approaches to taking creative chances.

UNIT ONE
THE HUMAN SIDE
OF RISK TAKING

IN THIS UNIT I describe as best I can how the human element affects risk taking, especially in the often thankless job of the middle manager. In some ways as little is known on the subject of risk taking as about the common cold. Actuarial risk in gambling and insurance, where odds are calculated on probability, has developed into a finely tuned technology. The whole theory of statistical probabilities (which governs even the weather report) continues to develop into a highly reliable science based on objective data.

But people are different. In groups, such as discussed in Chapter 4, they are somewhat predictable. As individuals, their personal motivations tend to create somewhat predictable styles, as seen in Chapter 3. But the more finite the population and subjective the situation, the less predictable the outcomes. Human behavior has predictability but it is based on nonmathematical skills. In this unit we will discuss risk as it relates to more subjective aspects of risk taking. The nature of this subjective risk is outlined in Chapter 1. Perhaps the basic rules of risk taking, as pointed up in Chapter 2, will give you a better self-understanding of why you zig when you should zag.

1 | The Nature of Risk Taking

IF YOU WERE TO WAKE UP one Monday morning and say, "I'm going to get more out of life," what would you mean? Would you withdraw your savings from the local savings and loan and invest in venture stocks, or perhaps go on a great vacation? Or do you mean you would become more self-directed? Would you perhaps decide to trust your intuitions or your relatives more? Would you no longer postpone confronting your boss about his recent negligence in some company project? Maybe you would take up tennis again, quit your job, get married to an old girl friend, eat a bigger breakfast than usual. Whatever your decision for how to obtain more out of life, risk and uncertainty are involved. This chapter outlines the nature of that risk.

THE NECESSITY OF CHANGE AND ITS SIDE EFFECTS

In the beginning God created constant change. Change accompanies health, vocation, maturing, reorganization, relationships, bus schedules, technology — all in all, our entire social fabric. Change is the way to describe the nature of the day. With it come risk and continual uncertainty.

For this book, written for middle managers, the words of John Gardner are important:

Today we can't afford not to take chances. I am always puzzled by people who talk as though advocates of change are just inventing ways to disturb the peace in what would otherwise be a tranquil community. We are not seeking change for the sheer fun of it. We must change to meet the challenge of altered circumstances. Change will occur whether we like it or not. It will be either change in a good and healthy direction or change in a bad and regrettable direction. There is no tranquility for us.[1]

I am now suggesting that there is no tranquility for middle managers. They are in need of understanding the nature of risk for each of them — thus strengthening themselves and their organizations, and planning how to handle the micro- as well as the macrochanges forced on them by a cheapened dollar, a fluctuating economy, a cultural rootlessness, a polluted environment, and giant everything.

Middle managers have in their hands the potential to influence the company. Whether an art director of an advertising firm, a GS 16 in a federal agency, a factory manager, a grocery chain manager, a sales manager, or a school principal — all can effect change if they will maximize opportunities for growth and move their organizations and their families toward greater wholeness, productivity, and satisfaction.

Let's examine how change increases risks for middle managers.

Age. First, change increases risk by making people older. At 40 a middle manager tends to consolidate gains rather than take new risks. A 40-year-old generally can't walk as fast, put in as many overtime hours, play tennis as well, or do any other activities that require the body to perform well. There is a reason why Johnny Unitas and George Blanda are heroes of professional football: They are old men; they are over 40.

Changes of heart. With three out of five marriages breaking up in the United States, there are many changes of heart. The breakups throw women and men on their own. Often with children, they now have to be both mother and father. This failure experience, combined with being 40, provides ever increasing uncertainty and risks in living.

Corporate fortunes. We are also affected quite beyond our control by corporate fortunes. For example, during the 1973 meat crisis, many small meat-packing houses had to close permanently. When the oil crisis came, independent gasoline stations were put out of business left and right. They didn't ask for change but it happened to them anyway.

Cultural changes. When the 1973 war in the Middle East broke out and President Nixon swore to protect Israel, I wondered who would protect my 15-year-old son from the President. The war, with its economic and emotional ramifications, suddenly put my son in the same jeopardy that had passed him by with peace in Vietnam. The culture, the country, the state, as well as various other institutions of authority, can place you in a high risk situation not of your choosing.

Survival of the fittest. Behind each middle manager is a newly trained person ready for the middle manager to die, be promoted, be fired, or otherwise disposed of. One personnel man I know never hires a Ph.D. in his department because he fears he will lose his own job. Of course, he will lose his job whether he brings in the Ph.D. or not. He can't prevent age, corporate fortunes, or a new style of management from dislodging him. There is always a rookie in the wings or a veteran from another team ready to take your place.

IDIOSYNCRATIC NATURE OF RISK

Risk taking, as we use it in this discussion, is idiosyncratic — idiosyncratic because we are talking about risk in relation to people. Unless you are discussing actuarial risk predicted by large numbers, you are in a world of uncertainty that is specific to each person, group, or institution — where risk is subjective, related to emotional climate of the specific environment, the types of people involved, and the stakes of the moment. Yes, there are mathematical models for decision making. Probabilities can be calculated for the number of deaths and births that will occur in the United States. But once you leave the world of the ordinal, risk becomes totally an eccentric matter, based on situational and subjective factors.

Differences Between People

Bear with me while I state the obvious, that there are significant differences between people. Although obvious, it also means that, given the same set of circumstances, two individuals have quite different levels of risk. If champion Bob Richards and I were to compete in a pole vaulting contest there would be some uncertainty regarding how well he would do. The uncertainty regarding my efforts would only be how badly I'd get hurt. In other words, his training, physical condition, and aptitude as opposed to mine reduce the uncertainty or risk that he takes.

Even though we know people are different, we still tend to compare one employee's performance with another's, just as we do one child's with another's. For example, "Look, Mary, even little Ann is willing to swim out over her head. Why aren't you?" Obviously because Mary assesses her risk as greater than little Ann's. A middle manager who apparently can't fire people is berated by the boss for not firing a particular thorny and unproductive employee. While the boss might not say it, chances are she is thinking, "Why can't Sam do what Tom does so well and easily?" Tom sees his risks and costs differently.

Perhaps the best definition, then, of risk taking is that it is the difference between your reach and your grasp. Stated in a textbook manner, "Risk is the uncertainty with respect to gain or loss for any person or company toward a particular opportunity." But I'm emphasizing that the actual or perceived grasp of the individual plays a great part in determining the risk level of any given opportunity.

Self-Perceptions

How one views oneself is a key to understanding why risk assessment is so idiosyncratic. Each of us views himself quite differently. Thus our assessment of our capacities often varies significantly from how others see us. For example, fourth-grade Johnny is asked to read aloud by the teacher. He knows Johnny can read, but he is not sensitive to how deeply convinced Johnny is that he can't read. Johnny's heart beats faster, his pupils distend, and a frog develops in his throat. He may know that he shouldn't feel that way, but to him the certainty of loss of face before his peers seems far to outweigh the gain of the teacher's approval. He, therefore, simply shakes his head negatively. The teacher gets angry or, perhaps, writes it off as Johnny's shyness, which, of course, may be true. The key to understanding the situation, however, is in understanding that Johnny, shy or not, felt his reach wasn't going to permit the grasp of success.

The strength of the self-image has been pointed up consistently by such writers as Carl Rogers,[2] S. I. Hayakawa,[3] and Karen Horney.[4] Each discusses the stability of the self-concept which is made up of elements of "me," "not me," and "wish it were me." Together, these elements form the self-concept that is much more of a "box" for the middle manager than the corporate one of "plateauing out," as suggested by Emanuel Kay.[5] The self-concept formed during the early years may have created a condition of self-administered plateauing out that prevents the middle manager from truly working to move up the hierarchy, much to the bewilderment of colleagues and superiors.

I'm reminded of the Saturday that my 12-year-old son wanted to know if the Vikings football team was going to play in Minneapolis or out of town. Most of us would seek the information from news sources. My son called Mick Tingelhoff, the Vikings' center, to ask him about the team's plans. Mick wasn't home but his gracious wife was, and she told him that the Vikings were to play in Chicago on Sunday. My son was gratified, I was bewildered by the direct approach, and my wife didn't know whether to be embarrassed or not.

My son has not yet labeled, stereotyped, and boxed in himself or others to such a degree that it causes self-limitations on going to an obvious source of information, someone he admired on the team. Most middle managers have built boxes around themselves that prevent deliberate choices that exceed their self-imposed boundaries called the self-concept. The balance of this book will spell out further what I think middle managers can and need to do. As Horney says, "For his well-functioning, man needs both the vision of possibilities, the perspective of the infinitude, and the realization of limitations, of necessities, of the concrete."[6]

Risk Taking as a Trait

Over the years people have said, "He's a risk taker," "She's never taken a risk in her life," or "I wish I were a risk taker." Today, behavioral science recognizes that risk is not a trait. In fact, a dramatic style of high or low risk is usually indicative of a fairly serious neurosis.[7] Risk taking in the healthy personality is always a function of the circumstances, alternatives available, and resources. Later on we will discuss the rules of risk taking, which, by their very existence, emphasize the rational and intuitive as determining how much risk one is willing to take.

Some years ago I described this phenomenon using a Kurt Lewin-like "field" description [8] that points up what I'm saying. That is, given circumstances as well as responses are conditioned by a number of factors, including physical and psychological needs, memories, values or religious commitment, self-concept, beliefs and expectations, and benefits and costs to other people. Depending on the circumstances, each of these factors has a positive or negative weight.

We are in that field of forces each time we face altered or about to be altered circumstances. The middle manager who is not boxed in by self-concept can then make better judgments about uncertainty as regards to loss or gain. However, this process is not all that simple. To say, "He's a risk taker" or "She plays it close to the vest," rather than being complimentary, may well be a simple diagnosis of a stabilized form of response to every circumstance based on poor consideration of what the ramifications of the choice would be.

RISK IS ALWAYS A FORM OF BETTING

Risk taking in any form is betting. Whether you are playing bingo, trading stocks, buying a car, passing another car on the highway, fighting a preventive war, starting your own business, or trying to maintain the status quo—these are all betting.

You bet either on yourself or on chance. Experiments by social scientists have indicated that people react quite differently when they are part of the equation. That is, such activities as betting on the roll of the dice, the numbers on a bingo card, the flip of a coin, or the skill of a mutual funds operator—all have an underlying theme: You have no direct chance to affect the outcome. The skill of others, combined with the odds, determines whether you win.

Many people would rather risk against the odds and keep

themselves out of the equation. They will bet great sums of money, or invest time trying to figure the odds, but in the final analysis — cheating being eliminated — the fates, or as we call it, the probabilities, determine the outcome. On the other hand, these same people may not bet on their golf game, start their own business, fly their own plane, bet on their horse, or bet on outcomes where their skill, luck, or ability are part of the equation.

In the laboratory setting the results quite obviously are different when the subject is asked to bet on a shuffleboard game he is playing versus the turn of a card. In this book we are more concerned with this latter kind of risk taking. A middle manager might win the Irish or New York sweepstakes and still not find personal gratification in using the money in satisfying ways. A middle manager may gamble away his salary but never bet on himself by taking organizational risks that would, in fact, help the organization.

An extension of betting on yourself is betting on others, a risky procedure but one with potentially beneficial results. Sven Lundstedt and John Lillibridge of Case Western Reserve University have developed a theory of interpersonal risk that involves a manager voluntarily giving away power and influence to employees.[9] They postulate that by so doing, the power shared with the staff may lead to cooperation, while the opposite form of behavior, reserving all power for oneself, leads to competition and conflict.

This concept of risk taking is important if you take power seriously. I do not think it explains or even seeks to understand the power of the supervisee. It does treat the manager as the string-puller, when, in fact, the people who pull are on both ends of the string. Of course, as part of a continuum of organizational style, as a middle manager, you may be more willing to share your authority with your subordinates when your boss does the same with you. You may not want to hear your boss saying to you, "What have you got, a committee running your shop?"

In other words, if you share your authority you want to take minimal organizational risks doing it. If it is the organizational style, then it's all right. However, in my experience, the most creative middle managers have usually taken clear organizational risks in this matter, often being far ahead of top management. They take these risks because they believe that higher production will result. Lillibridge and Lundstedt maintain that "men in high producing departments, in contrast with men in low, feel that more influence is exercised at every hierarchical level." [10]

DYNAMIC VERSUS STATIC RISK

I've borrowed the terms "dynamic" and "static" from the field of risk management in insurance. Other than the area of mathematics, the insurance industry has conceptualized more about risk than any other practical discipline. According to insurance people, *dynamic* risks are those related to managerial, innovative, and political risks. We discuss these more specifically in Chapter 9. The other class of risk is *static* risk, which relates only to potential losses. The risk management consultant helps clients examine their potential losses. Where they can't get someone to cover, share, or otherwise reduce them, clients are encouraged to protect themselves by insurance.

Most of us are willing to discuss or bet on ways that will minimize our losses. Thus, a bureaucrat may avoid making decisions, touch all bases before acting, never say yes only say no, only take positions that are just under the person who has final authority, increase staff and acquire more functions when not really necessary or appropriate, and protect the boss at all costs.[11]

Whether deserved or not, the general stereotyped image of middle managers is that they are only interested in minimizing losses, dealing with static risk. Top management, on the other hand, is more often seen as dealing with dynamic risk through maximizing opportunities. Dynamic risk is risking the loss of something certain for the gain of something uncertain. This in no way implies that uncertainty is meant to be nebulous, undefined, or just a guess. It simply means that, figuratively speaking, I place a chip on a number risking its loss for the potential gain of a 20-to-1 payoff. In static risk I simply would never put the chip on a number. Effective management is always risking the investor's dollar in new ventures, new organizations, or revisions of past dollar-makers. Every management decision has the element of dynamic risk governed only by the practical rules of risk taking.

Chapter 1 describes the nature of risk for the middle manager. Risk is the outgrowth of change, the only constant factor in our world today. The question is never, "Should we change?" but "In what direction?" Change increases risk for the middle manager in a number of ways. Changes in age, changes in one's personal life, changes in corporate fortunes, and so on—all influence the middle manager's ability to risk.

Risk taking is defined in this chapter as the difference between your reach and your grasp. It all boils down to, "How far are you willing to leave that secure seat on the ground to get that apple in the tree?" Risk is an idiosyncratic thing, very dependent on the actual differences between people and their differing self-perceptions. As we will learn in this unit, each person assesses the odds and the cost for each situation in a different way. Each is influenced by the field of forces that surrounds risk taking in a singular fashion.

One constant factor in risk taking is that it is always a form of betting. You bet either on yourself or on chance. Which you choose is a key to the kind of risk taker you are. Some of us like to step out of the picture altogether and bet on other people's skills or on some kind of probability risk. Others prefer only to bet where they can influence the outcome. This last kind of betting is our concern in this book. This is the kind of risk that can change a middle manager's life.

One aspect of this organizational risk taking was defined by Lundstedt and Lillibridge in the theory of interpersonal risk. This theory states that a manager may voluntarily give away power and influence to subordinates in order to increase cooperation and production. This kind of behavior treats seriously the desire employees have to affect in some way the workings of the organization. The parceling out of power is a big risk for most middle managers. It may not fit in with the organization's style, and it will most certainly cause comment in the beginning—most of it not favorable. The results, however, are all to the organization's benefit: in increased production and morale and decreased destructive competition.

The final concept presented in this chapter is that of dynamic versus static risk. Dynamic risks are those taken to make gains. Static risks are those taken to protect against loss. Actually, static risks are more often an avoidance of risk rather than an effort to risk. This is an important concept, perhaps more important as a philosophical foundation for this book than as a description of phenomena. Middle managers usually follow static risk patterns. A large part of this book is concerned with changing that image to one of dynamic risk takers. Remember, change is inevitable. The direction of change is the only concern. I want to show you ways to change that will help you become more creative and bring you closer to achieving your potential.

2 | Rules of Risk Taking

CHAPTER 1 communicated that we can't talk about risk unless we also talk about opportunity. In other words, how you deal with the uncertainty around an opportunity is how you take or don't take risks. Opportunities come in all sizes, shapes, and colors. Some risks, of course, are those related to making a decision. You may have to recommend dropping a product or a program that others think important. You may have to fire someone or spend buy-in money to get into an unproven market.

Other opportunities will be more personal or involve interpersonal relationships. You may be asked to be an adversary witness in the divorce of some friends. You may be confronted with the necessity to back your boss's misrepresentation. You may have ethical choices: you, a male, may want to travel with your female secretary on your next trip. You may have an illegal chance to exercise your option before your company's stock advances.

The list is infinite in type and number. Each day brings both the dynamic risk, where loss and gain are pitted against one another, and the static risk, where the opportunity may simply be to consolidate and protect present gains. Your only assurance is that every day something will turn up. What can you use to guide your responses to these opportunities?

If people were truly rational creatures, the balance of this chapter—with the three simple rules of risk taking—would do away with the need for the rest of the book. These rules are simple, straightforward, and sensible. But where the breakdown occurs, of course, is in their application, since what determines our risk-taking behavior is more often than not that part of us that is irrational, devious, and unconscious. Risk taking, by defi- nition, is dealing with the uncertain, whereas logic and order are more easily applied to the certain.

Accepting these limitations on the usefulness of the three rules, let's outline them and do our best to see how they work.

NEVER RISK MORE THAN YOU CAN AFFORD TO LOSE

An obvious statement, but deceptively simple. The amount you can afford to lose is determined by very subjective criteria. For example, you may be forced to state your limit in arbitrary terms prior to a trip to Las Vegas. Most people who go to Las Vegas on the free trips sponsored by casinos establish their credit before they go and then preset a limit on what they will lose. Their casino will not advance them chips or money beyond that arbitrary limit. Some years ago, Frank Sinatra became frus- trated when a Las Vegas casino sought to prevent him from los- ing more than he had stated he could afford to lose prior to com- ing to the casino.

In other words, in the heat of the moment of taking risks we are not able to decide rationally what we can afford to lose. Irrationality has great influence on each of us in uncertain situa- tions. The subjective element in us automatically ups our chances for error, and that ever present uncertainty about the future makes our judgment of the amount we can afford to lose in the present quite relative.

In an objective, dynamic risk situation related to financial involvement, two people in the same financial circumstances might well decide quite differently what they can afford to lose. One manager, who I consider quite well-off and in no imminent danger of financial collapse, told me I wouldn't be able to under- stand why he couldn't take advantage of a certain opportunity. He said he had never been without an adequate and very comfortable living, while he knew I had had less than comfortable experiences while a youngster. He said, "You know that you can live without money. I'm not at all sure that I can." In other words, in considering the same opportunity, we each saw what we could afford to lose quite differently. The bottom of my barrel was considerably deeper than his.

Subjective confusion is in the nature of the word "risk" itself. Is telling it like it is riskier or less risky than keeping your mouth shut in a tense situation at work? How can you determine how much you have to lose either way? If you are open in a highly volatile situation, you may be severely reprimanded, distrusted, or even fired. If you say nothing, you may be seen as weaseling, weak, and not capable of higher responsibility. Of course, the values of your superiors, the social norms of the organization, and your own values have a considerable effect on your decision. I simply want to point out how complex it is for all of us to determine how much we can afford to lose at any time, and then to determine which choice will lose us the least or gain us the most.

This discussion regarding the subjective factors in determining what one can afford to lose is meaningful, especially for middle managers, who tend to exaggerate their potential and actual losses. That is, they tend to see the glass half empty rather than half full. A good illustration of the need to gain perspective is one boy's first lesson in gambling at a county fair. He was intrigued by a little game where a ball hung on a string beside a bowling pin on the bar of one of the carney stands. The object was simply to swing the ball so that it would swing around the pin from his side and knock the pin down as it came back toward him. It seemed simple. The carney did it effortlessly several times. It appeared to the boy that for 25 cents and a chance to win a panda for the young lady with him he couldn't afford to pass up the opportunity. Just as you might guess, the carney doubled the odds, so that it was always double or nothing until, beet-red, the young man had donated 16 dollars, had a serious loss of face, and lost his carfare and the ability to buy his date something to eat. Apparently, he lost more than he could afford to lose.

The question is, did he really risk more than he could afford to lose? Of course he did, but not in the long run. He learned volumes about opportunities, carneys, himself, and so on. The actual payoff was a burning experience which made him wary of opportunities in which he has so little influence over the basic control of the odds. He also learned, in retrospect, that he didn't really risk more than he could afford to lose, although at the time it certainly felt like it.

In other words, your historical perspective on yourself, your talents, your responsibilities, and so forth may be inhibiting and cause you to take fewer risks today. Why? Because you think a potential loss may be more than you can afford to lose when in reality you will get through it, learn from it, and begin again. Middle managers are not likely to bet their last 16 dollars because they would feel that was more than they could afford to lose. If, however, their self-esteem were higher and their self-confidence stronger, their perspective would be quite different. As Dr. Art Coombs, an advocate of the school of perceptive psychology, often says, "There is a fine line between a threat and a challenge." The opportunity is a threat to those who predict failure and a challenge to those who think they might win. The middle manager is apt to be threat-prone, given an opportunity involving personal risk. Being threat-prone makes him magnify potential losses and minimize potential gains.

Let's examine a company situation that illustrates the intertwinement of personal and organizational risks involved in responding to daily opportunities. An electronics firm had several divisions, all with somewhat independent charters. The larger divisions annually invested money from their profits in various applied research groups within the company for the development of new technologies. One of these research groups began to manufacture and market certain components that another division, interested in selling systems, wanted to use at its option. The components represented 70 percent of the particular system the division was selling. The division and the research group would trip over each other in the marketplace, one selling components and the other a system. They had other working relationships where a particular component was a much smaller proportion of the system. In these cases, there were only minor abrasions. In the situation in question, however, there was clearly a market for the components but not as clear a market for the system surrounding it, causing a major collision of self-interests.

The conflict is simple, but just watch the plot thicken. Remember, the systems division was giving part of its profits to the research group. The research group had long since decided to become self-supporting, and needed to get sales on this component to reduce dependency on the divisions. The systems division wanted the company to move the employees and production facilities of the components out of the research group into its division. The research group complained that the systems people were so few that it made more sense to move them into the component subgroup within the research group. In the meantime, they were bad-mouthing each other in the marketplace.

It was then proposed that key people from each group work together to find a reasonable solution, or solutions, to the problem. It was observed that at the present rate of accelerated hostility, they could hurt each other mortally. Neither could afford to lose that much. However, as they came together to find a solution, many risks popped up for each side. If research incorporated the systems people, systems, which was already struggling to keep above the waterline, would lose many of its key staff and perhaps go under. Research, on the other hand, without the component to manufacture, could not become an independent operating division and would be relegated to a small applied research group once again, losing its chances for upward mobility.

The battle was too risky, and for either to lose would cost more than either, individually or corporately, could afford. They both needed something less risky than any of the alternatives mentioned — perhaps a joint study group under a jointly selected person from corporate staff, more joint marketing attempts, more personal openness. Or perhaps in the future the research group could broaden its support base enough to be able to release its hold on the components, or the systems group could become a recognized competitor of other major systems groups with many more systems to offer than it presently had. Then, at that time, a decision over who gets the baby could be made. Now, though, neither group could afford to risk giving their product away, nor could they afford open fighting in the marketplace. There was just too much to lose.

You can see yourself on either side, scrambling for your own future, identifying with the good guys and seeking to reduce your own risks, but seeing no way not to increase others' risks while reducing yours. There is no way to divorce your personal and subjective risks from the corporate, objective risk. Every opportunity creates both money and value conflicts that must be considered.

In summary, then, the first rule of risk taking, while easy to understand, is more difficult to apply, since we all define "how much I can afford to lose" in a very subjective way. It is also impossible to divorce personal stakes from the corporate betting on the come. Middle managers need to fully incorporate that thought in order to fathom the sometimes unconsciously devious moves of executive management.

In determining the amount of risk you can afford to take, keep the following guidelines in mind:

Plan ahead. Set your personal limits and stick by them. Don't be pushed beyond what you decided to do before the crunch. There will be another hour, another day, another year. Don't be panicked into under- or overrisking.

Get advice from people who have no stake in the outcome except for what happens to you. Always take into consideration their own success at taking risks.

Don't use other people as an excuse for inaction. For example, I can't afford to lose because my son wouldn't be able to go to college, or my wife couldn't have a car, or my friends wouldn't like it. It may be true, but these excuses are just another way of saying you are afraid.

Have alternatives. Always try to develop alternatives — another job, another income, a backup choice.

DON'T RISK A LOT FOR A LITTLE

Again, this rational, believable statement is compromised with the restrictive words "lot" and "little." Both must be subjectively defined by each person using his or her supposedly objective criteria. To get a better picture of this problem, let's consider some descriptions where risking a lot may be asked for a little in return.

One example is the constant temptation of a man or woman,

married and in love with a person who would be hurt by infidelity, who nevertheless takes an occasional roll in the hay, hoping the spouse will never find out. Here is an example of what subjective criteria can do to you. In the passion of the moment, one may say it was risking a little for a lot. From my point of view, the temporary investment in the one and the long-term investment in the other are risks in just the opposite way. Maybe you reject my criteria. In any case, it is quickly evident that one person's "little" is another person's "lot."

In the presidential race between Richard Nixon and George McGovern, many calculated risks were taken. Perhaps the worst faux pas was that of Watergate itself. It seemed beyond the average person's understanding that one political party's goon squad would actually burglarize the headquarters of another. There seemed to be so little potential gain. But getting caught and exposed as burglars certainly had serious implications as to the lengths Nixon's associates would go to insure his election.

Another related example is a presidential aide discussing with the presiding judge in the Ellsberg case the position of FBI director. This, in the midst of the trial. Because the government had burglarized Ellsberg's physician's office and otherwise shown dramatic concern with extreme conflict with *The New York Times* over Ellsberg, the discussion with the judge seemed an obvious attempt to apply excessive influence. To what end? Again, the second rule of risk taking was violated — don't risk a lot for a little.

Ellsberg and his associates were also risk takers for releasing the now famous Pentagon Papers. The same is true of the publishers of *The New York Times* and *Los Angeles Times* and the *Washington Post*. They risked a lot, including a confrontation with the Office of the President, with only the courts between them and a loss of their rights to freely publish. Obviously, they thought they were risking a great deal, but for a great deal as well.

Now consider the rule's application in more business-like circumstances. Assume there is constant tension between you and your boss; no matter what you do, nothing goes right. You can, of course, fight her on every issue, but you build a stereotype of troublemaker or sexist with her that prevents you from getting heard on the issues where your stake is highest. Your generalized need to demonstrate that you aren't dominated by her robs you of the influence that you and your associates need, and want you to have, in the decision-making process. You risk a lot for a little.

As an applied behavioral science consultant, I have been called upon to initiate the changing of an organization's social norms of mistrust, minimal communication, and authoritarian decision making. At first, I was willing to sit with a president and his vice presidents for a weekend to carefully lead them through the prickly paths of greater candor to more genuine levels of communication—the beginning of the change process. However, I soon found that not all presidents, general managers, and so on were good guys. Some smiled and put up with what was said by their colleagues, but didn't ask me back, and, subsequently, would subtly punish their colleagues. Other groups of managers strongly resisted greater openness with each other and with their boss. Individually, they would confess to me that they wanted more free-flowing communication, but, as one man put it, "You're only here for the weekend. We're the ones who stay on living with the consequences of what we say."

They were right, of course. Because I was being paid to, and because I believed in the essential healthiness of greater openness, I was asking them to risk a lot for a little. They were only promised whatever might be the residual results of a candid weekend. That was hardly an appropriate reward for managers who were frightened, at the very least, of hurting each other's feelings irreparably, and, at the most, of reprisals by boss or peers.

This insight led me to demand greater commitment before beginning a change process. In effect, I wanted the boss to demonstrate that the stakes were high and that his intention was long-range change. As a result, he could ask for as well as take more risks of being open when the opportunity presented itself. The potential loss was balanced by the potential of greater gain.

Perhaps the greatest risk the middle manager takes is pulling the rule book on the boss. If this is done, it had better be for maximum benefit of the person or the organization, never for petty reasons. I know of a government agency where a director of personnel resented that his boss was younger and less qualified for his job than was the personnel director himself, who had been passed over for the position. He dealt with his feelings toward the boss by responding to unusual requests with a "No, it can't be done." If his boss wanted to trade slots, he refused to approve it. If a senator wanted a constituent put at the top of a waiting list, the personnel director refused — not, mind you, on moral grounds, but because he wanted to cause his boss embarrassment and bureaucratic pain. It did not take long for his boss to decide that the personnel director could be of more assistance to another agency. Once again, a lot was risked for a petty little.

The most foolish of risks are those taken by such public figures as Jimmy Hoffa, Billy Sol Estes, and many others we all could name. These men, often brilliant and respected, stole or otherwise used their influence in criminal ways for very little long-range return. Then there are others whose style of risk taking, although along quite different lines and with different goals, is similar. Consider Joe Kapp, former Patriot quarterback, who held out for a particular contract and never played again. The same is true for Denny McLain, former pitcher for Detroit, who couldn't accept personal discipline. He pitches in the minors today. In their success, they lost perspective on the relationship between loss and gain. Each one, in his own way, risked a lot for a little.

The danger for middle managers tends to be of the opposite kind. They often think that any risk is too much for any return. Because they focus on static risks, protecting their gains, they actually risk the future by not taking any risks in the present. An inflexible value system, a reflexive approach to problem solving, and a consistently cautious manner are also forms of risking a lot for a little — the "little" being some immediate security and the "lot" being the rest of your life. There are few stories of middle managers not taking risks. The reason is that there is little of newsworthiness in such nonaction.

Perhaps the most notorious group of middle managers in regard to a consistent low or no-risk position is the corporate training department. While one doesn't like stereotyping any corporate group, it is known that few people in training departments are ready to take the risks necessary to develop innovative programs with the potential of giving people the opportunity to say they don't like what is happening "even if it is good for me."

These training managers, often bright and concerned people, look for predictable training packages, and, as one impressive assistant vice president in a bank said, try to keep the boat from rocking. Executive management often expects training and personnel primarily to keep the workers off its back. Thus training people will risk becoming political survivors with innocuous programs and acting as window dressing for the corporation's image of being concerned about people.

The second rule of risk taking can be violated several ways. It can be violated by your glands, by your need to prove something to yourself quite apart from your potential loss, by behavioral scientists encouraging you to risk blindly, by your need to punish, by your misperception of yourself as being outside the rules of ordinary people, and by doing nothing.

To prevent risking a lot for a little, you should *avoid taking risks for punitive reasons.* Don't stick your neck out to hurt someone else. Even if they do get hurt, so will you.

Don't take risks to avoid losing face. From childhood we often fear not taking a dare. When you say you'd do something that later turns out to be riskier than the returns the practical result will bring, forget it. Let the observers find someone else to bait. Nothing is worse than a group urging two boys to mix it up, with neither wanting to fight. Both fear a loss of face and will risk getting their heads bashed in to please the onlookers.

Don't take risks purely for reasons of principle. For example, telling your boss he's a lousy supervisor has little merit if it's done simply because one ought to be open with one's boss. Some people, such as Jourard in *The Transparent Self,*[1] suggest that emotional health is correlated with constant openness. Perhaps for Jourard this is true, because he is sheltered by tenure in a state university. Openness for its own sake is irrational and can lead to risking a lot for a little. Of course, having the ability to be open selectively is part of being healthy. But irrational risk taking hardly argues for emotional health or a full stomach.

CONSIDER THE ODDS AND YOUR INTUITION

For the purposes of this section, let's forget pure gambling situations. McClelland, in *The Achieving Society,*[2] and Kogan and Wallach, in *Risk Taking,*[3] as well as Atkinson, in his journal reports,[4] tell us we are dealing with two types of risk phenomena. One kind of risk taking is taking a chance on pure probabilities. The other is betting on one's skill. They demonstrate that the same people behave quite differently under these two sets of conditions. For example, managers with high needs to achieve avoid gambling where they have little control of the outcome. They may gamble but only under the very best of odds.

Odds, except in an actuarial sense, become subject to most of our fears and neuroses. Let me share an old experience that illustrates the nature of the trouble in irrationally considering the odds. It happened one Christmas season when a friend was playing in a dance orchestra in a Florida nightclub. The piano player became ill, and a new one was requested from the secretary of the musician's local. He promptly sent a man who drove a hearse in which he kept a spinet piano and a bed. An intriguing person, to say the least. Besides being a good piano player, he also loved to gamble and felt he had several excellent systems that worked under all conditions. While gambling was illegal in Florida, the management was able, mostly through monthly presents to the county sheriff's office, to keep a card game going. The band was aware that the game was fixed, with all but one or two players being shills for the house. In addition, it was known that marked cards were being used. The piano player knew all of this. He knew the odds, and yet each night, on every break and until late in the morning, he gambled against the shills and the dealer. Most nights he lost badly.

As we see, even when the odds were clear, some compulsive pattern pulled our friend to the gambler's table. He always said "Tonight's the night!"

In *Risk Taking* Kogan and Wallach discuss at some length the irrationality of many who bet on their ability in a particular skill test. They demonstrate that those who bet on themselves in more rational ways, situation by situation, do consider the odds each time, unlike our piano player. Those who are consistently high risk takers become even higher with losses or when the odds get longer. It is as if they must prove some sort of omnipotence to overcome their feeling of powerlessness. Those who are consistently low risk takers, conversely, bet low and drop out quickly when losing or when the odds lengthen.

Neither Wallach and Kogan, Atkinson, nor McClelland discusses intuition much, which is both surprising and depressing because of its obvious influence on risk taking. There is no question that the key to considering the odds lies in putting it all together and making a judgment which may not appear to be supported by the facts. The following is a quick and simple way to illustrate what I mean. Please don't take the numbers too seriously. They are not the products of research. They represent ratios derived from observing managers for some years.

Take the two factors of probability and intuition. If the probabilities are known and look good or so-so and your intuition says you can bring it off, then chances are nine out of ten you will succeed. If the probabilities are unknown but your intuition tells you to go ahead, the odds are better than average. If the probabilities are obvious but your intuition draws a blank, the odds are still in favor of taking the risk. If the odds are unknown and your sense of what is right isn't forthcoming, then the odds are definitely against you (see Figure 1).

The problem with most middle managers is that, when computing the odds and risk, they leave out one factor—the person making the judgment. Just as Einstein demonstrated, that the observer affects what is observed, so the risk taker affects the risk or the judgment regarding the risk. The phenomenon is simi-

Probabilities

	Known	Unknown
Active	Success Odds 90/10	Success Odds 60/40
Inactive	Success Odds 60/40	Success Odds 10/90

Intuition (row label spanning Active / Inactive)

Figure 1. Probability and intuition affecting the odds.

lar to a police department calculating the odds of a riot at a basketball game without taking into consideration the deterring or inciting effect of its presence.

The manager who calculates the odds for and against asking for a raise or promotion may take everything into consideration except his own actual value to the company. You are factor X in every opportunity. If you don't push executive management, if you allow yourself to be emasculated, your integrity frayed by years of saying yes when you mean no, then the odds will consistently be against your success on any given opportunity. For you, considering the odds may simply be another way of saying "I can't do it!" The problem is you—your overriding needs, fears, qualms, and general lack of self-assurance.

In this chapter we discussed three rules to consider when taking risks, as well as a few of the reasons why those rules are impossible to apply in any consistent fashion. Rules imply that risk taking follows some kind of lawful pattern, whereas risk taking really deals with the uncertain, the irrational. Thus our three rules are really guidelines. The greater the certainty with which we apply these guidelines the less the outcome is a risk and the more it is merely a logical conclusion.

The first rule is *never risk more than you can afford to lose*. You can determine that amount of allowable risk, insofar as it can really be determined, by planning ahead, by getting advice from others, by having alternatives, and by not using other people as excuses for inaction. You must consider risk on both personal and corporate levels, since the two are inseparable in controlling your fate.

The second rule is *don't risk a lot for a little*. This is as subjective as the first, and equally impossible to follow concretely. It means exercising some control over your emotions in a risk situation. It means carefully identifying what is a risk, a loss, or a gain. Three ways to keep from breaking this rule are to avoid taking risks for punitive reasons, to avoid taking risks to keep from losing face, and to avoid taking risks purely for reasons of principle.

The third rule is *consider the odds and your intuition*. Take yourself into account, since you, as a risk taker, influence the risk and the outcome. Remember there is a difference between taking a chance where you have no control over the odds and risking in a situation where you are a factor with some weight. Work each situation on its own merits. Don't let a past history of risking stifle your intuitive decisions or prevent you from seeing that the odds are in your favor. Know your own value to yourself and to the company. Explore your feelings around a risk to be taken and jump accordingly.

3 | What Inhibits Risk Taking?

LET'S PUT IT INTO ONE WORD—fear. We are all afraid, and we have a right to be. We are born little, helpless, and naked, and into an environment we didn't choose. We have a limited amount of mental and physical equipment which is yet to be developed. We may be loved, hated, or ignored as children. Most of the time we experience all three. Fate and accidents often seem to control our destiny. These experiences are added to the peculiar genetic formation that is us, as well as the particular history of how we integrate it all. In addition, there is a built-in disintegration process accompanying our lives. That's me, that's you—unique and motivated by many singular factors.

However, one motivational factor common to us all is fear. The biggest fears that drive us are those of failure, of what other people will think, and of uncertainty. McClelland, in *The Achieving Society,* speaks of these, conversely, as the needs to achieve, to affiliate, and to have power. I like the negative way of describing these variables as fears because it better predicts the crazy actions we sometimes take. For example, a college student with a high fear of failure, or what psychologists call test anxiety, may not even be able to take a test for which he has adequately prepared. Or he might act impulsively and take a test for which he was not at all prepared. In neither case was he responding to the opportunity by risking what he could afford to lose, not

31

risking a lot for a little, nor considering the odds and his intuition. He was simply motivated by fear, fear of failure.

FEAR OF FAILURE

Excessive fear of failure prevents us from setting our goals at realistic levels of risk. A good example of how fear affects goal setting is in trying to implement the management system called management by objectives. The process is simple. Ideally, everyone sets his or her goals, which may or may not be agreed to by the supervisor. After appropriate negotiation, final goals are established, methods spelled out, and the employee, supposedly, is freer to pursue the designated objectives.

Presumably, then, all the individual goals will finally interlock, and in some wondrous way the whole organization will move forward in a collective consciousness toward the larger goal, which is more than the sum of the individual goals. Ideally, excellent! In practice, its application is less than ideal. Why? Consider that people who like to measure and be measured have established the system for people who don't like it and who have excessive fear of failure—often middle managers. Middle managers are always the ones who are responsible for installation of the system. Top management decrees; middle management implements. Most often, this is where the process breaks down.

Executive management sets broad, abstract goals. The concrete risk taking must come from the middle managers. However, you'll recall that I previously described middle managers as having a static rather than dynamic approach to risk taking. In other words, when they look at the new system they only see another way to prove themselves failures. Adding insult to injury, they are told they must also establish the criteria by which they will then prove this worst of all possibilities.

In therapy, this is referred to as a double bind, or damned if they do and damned if they don't. If they set their goals too high, they will surely fail. If they set them too low and surpass them, they will still see themselves as failures because the goals weren't set high enough. Most middle managers avoid the bind by developing a quite unconscious resistance to being involved in the system at all. Dates for reviews slip, slip, and slip again. Interviews with employees at first occur but soon disappear. Everyone gets "too busy" with the job to carry on with the program. The only people who cooperate are those who have a need to achieve and therefore want a report card to show at the end of the reporting period. There are just enough of these people to keep the system looking like it's half working.

There are also enough bosses pushing for the system who can't wait for Junior to bring home bad grades. Bad grades on objectives give the manager an opportunity to play "Now I've got you" with the subordinate, based on the fact that the subordinate "didn't even do what he himself said he would do."

There is another, somewhat perverse, way of expressing fear of failure which was introduced to me by M. Robert Wilson, M.D., director of the Constance Bultman Wilson Center for Education and Psychiatry.[1] He interprets excessive fear of performance measures and high achievement in some adolescents as fear of success rather than fear of failure. The bright adolescent who refuses to accept responsibility for himself or for anyone else may really fear that once successful at it, he will be required to be independent. This adolescent may have such needs to be dependent that he will seriously resist becoming well—that is, becoming independent, letting others depend on him, and being held accountable.

If we apply the same philosophy to middle managers, it becomes obvious why many resist goal setting and high achievement, even the brightest ones or the ones with promise. They fear success, not failure. Indeed, if they achieved the high goals they set, they might be promoted out of middle management, be given more responsibility, and have to set even higher goals and have to hold increasing numbers of people responsible for their own goals. Because they have not worked through their adolescent development task of independence versus dependence, they are afraid of the independence that success would bring to them. As it is, having only intermediate responsibility, they can place the blame on the decision makers above them. They can bravely say, "If I were running this place. . . ." In fact, the idea of running the place, having the last word, being the person where the buck stops, strikes panic in their hearts. These people often have a real need to remain dependent. Thus it is difficult to know whether it is fear of failure or fear of success that motivates people to avoid standards and specific goals.

Fear of failure, or success in this case, appears in many guises. One of the more day-to-day occurrences concerns changing jobs, vocations, or organizations. If we believe the papers, HEW reports, and our friends, most people don't like their work. Is this dislike simply a symptom of insecurity in our times? Or is it that people really would prefer a class society with limitations on what was expected from each of them? I'm not sure of the answer to the question, but when a middle manager in an engineering firm begins discussing with me why he can't leave his job for one he really wants, the reasons often sound manufactured. He blames it on age, children's education, need for security, and a dozen other reasons. I'm certain that while he may be only partially succeeding at his present vocation, just the thought of a change raises the hideous specter of potential failure.

A few years ago the president of a small manufacturing firm that made a product unchallenged by serious competitors asked for and received help to develop his best middle management. This was a family-owned company in which the owner had become chairman of the board, and a trusted officer was made president. Most of the executive management were just learning what budgets were all about, but the president saw them becoming increasingly effective through previous experiences in organization development. On the other hand, middle management was made up of men who had been with the company for many years and had held relatively the same jobs. Some had worked for the company as students and later became full-time employees. None of them had been exposed to the new approach to management improvement called organizational development.

Several approaches were suggested for middle manager training. The one selected was to train all middle managers between the foreman and corporate officer levels in values and styles of management espoused by advocates of organizational development. A three-phase program was developed. The first phase was specifically an introduction for some 25 middle managers. The second was a consolidation of learnings, and the third was the integration of middle with executive management.

During the first phase, several significant symptoms of unsurfaced morale problems appeared. First of all, the group entered the experience already hostile, believing that all executive management wanted was a new way to manipulate them. This was not totally surprising, because I can say, without exception, that for the past seven years every organization I've contracted — government, business, or volunteer — more often than not middle managers have been suspicious, hostile, disbelieving, and downright mulish when it came to getting their attention.

The second striking feature occurred during a money exercise. The exercise involved groups of three people, each of whom had donated five dollars to the kitty and who jointly had to decide which two of the three would get the fifteen dollars. There were three rules: The decision could not be made by chance, no deals could be made for later division of the spoils, and all three had to agree on which two would get the money. The object of the exercise was to provide a situation that would help people examine their values, especially regarding giving, taking, and receiving, and the risks inherent in each. With our assistance, they could gain self-insight into their customary behavioral patterns on the job.

The group was asked to perform the exercise twice. The second time proved a real eye-opener, for now people began to open up and say why they needed the money. Those who were already down five dollars were now threatened by the loss of another five. There were serious pleas for the money based on such statements as, "I haven't taken my wife out to supper in six months because I don't have ten extra dollars to spend." Soon it became apparent that many of the participants were on salaries that were indecent for the responsibilities they had been given, in a company which annually produced more than a 30 percent return on its investment. For the first time there was real openness and sharing of concerns among these middle managers. The result was a direct appeal by them to executive management — although they wanted the consultants to request it — for a salary survey and appropriate adjustment. The consultants encouraged them to risk making demands of executive management. Executive management was very responsive in this case.

Now why would these people stay in jobs which cause them such shame? What is in the makeup of such people that plants their feet as if in concrete year after year? Is it fear of failing elsewhere? Is it fear of success and the attendant responsibility? We could well ask, "So, what's wrong with failing? People do it every day." The middle manager with a superabundance of fear can't take it that easily. She often internalizes and personalizes every failure. In psychiatric terms, she introjects, that is, assumes total responsibility. Knowing that they will fail and hating themselves for it, these types of middle managers avoid situations where they may fail, thereby avoiding dynamic risk opportunities. Conversely, they might deal with the situation by blaming external forces—the boss, the times, the situation—accepting no personal responsibility. Psychiatrists call this projection. In either case, one avoids opportunities which cause pain and potential shame, and that is what failure becomes inside. Nothing is more degrading than the feeling of shame.

The purpose of this book is not to probe the personal history (were it possible) of each of you but rather to spell out the consequences of your fears and to assure you that they are generic to us all. Later, ways are outlined to practice reducing the controlling effect of such fears. If, however, my self-directed remedies don't work, you should hightail it to a trained mental health worker and get help. Again, it is a double bind for you. What if you risk going for help and you fail to improve? All you've done is to create another source of shame. Complicated as it is, only you can break the circle. Executive management isn't responsible for your mental health. You are. There's nothing wrong with failing. Some of my best friends do it. There is something wrong, however, with letting your fear of failure cause you shame, govern your life, prevent you from setting realistic goals, changing jobs, or leaving a low-paying situation, or make you blame everyone else for your fear.

FEAR OF WHAT PEOPLE WILL THINK

Theoretically, one of the great values for people attending sensitivity training is a greater sensitivity to and an awareness of others' needs and feelings. I want to emphasize *self*-awareness in those areas.

For one person, the first human relations laboratory he ever attended surprised him, but not because of <u>how much more</u> <u>sensitized he became to others' feelings and needs.</u> On the contrary, he became increasingly aware then, and in subsequent years, of <u>how sensitive he already was to what others thought</u> of <u>him.</u> He had learned from an overly sensitive mother to care excessively about his effect on her and on others as well. Without intending to, she made him a walking radio tower, picking up signals to adapt him to what was required for success. Mixed in this sour apple pie were a few stringy raisins which became the seed of a later ego development—one much less dependent on what others thought of him or his actions. However, in the interim this excessive concern for what others thought created a fear of not being accepted and, therefore, of working in relationships for acceptance above all else. These fears prevented him from taking appropriate risks.

Carl Rogers describes this condition as defensiveness, R. W. White calls it defensive inhibition, and Sigmund Freud calls it repression and denial. Of course, the defensive person might well include in the excessive concern for his appearance a risky or conservative posture consistent with that image. Thus, you have Evel Knievel constantly seeking new ways to confirm himself as a man of courage, or the professional football player risking his body and life each week. I'm neither of these and most of us aren't. You and I are more cautious as a result of our consuming preoccupation with our image. We need affiliation, approval, buddy-buddy relationships—and then we hate how they control our choices.

This attitude starts early with the edict in kindergarten that we have to share. Since you want to avoid disapproval, you share, even when you hate every minute of it. You and the teacher and your playmates all beam approval, but somehow you aren't satisfied as you sit by the sandbox, impatiently waiting for that redhead's turn to end so you can grab that toy again. But, remember, if you don't do it politely and demonstrate that you are taking her feelings into account, you may rate disapproval once more. As McClelland says, "In more other-directed countries (such as the U.S.A.) stress on self-realization is checked and disciplined by much practice in learning to be sensitive to the opinions of others through participation in group activities." [2] Conferences, committees, and extracurricular activities socialize us quite early. The deepest scars on our souls are often those received from wounds inflicted by playground associates in team sports.

Testing programs contribute to the fear we have of being unacceptable. Is there anyone who can say that, when he takes the Minnesota Multiphasic Personality Inventory, the Edwards' Personal Preference Scale, the Strong Vocational Interest Blank, or any of the hundreds of other attitudinal, intelligence, or psychopathology-oriented tests, he isn't fearful? In this case fear is a perfectly reasonable reaction. Once again you are faced with the possible rejection of that golden image, or the confirmation of that jaded image, you have of yourself. The very fact that you accept the "right" of a prospective employer to examine your personality structure is an indication of how far you are willing to go to please. You can only hope that the employer finds you to his liking.

Another part of my life includes being a psychotherapist to young people in a center for education and psychiatry. One young man, dropped from college for stealing, using hallucinogenic drugs, and receiving low grades, was all set to enter the institution. On the eve of his arrival, his father called to cancel the appointment. He had decided to send his son to Detroit to work in a factory "until he straightened himself out," presumably by himself. It seems that the Eagleton affair during the 1972 presidential election had reminded the father that his son might be ruined by having on his record that he had attended a center such as ours. Isn't this a sign of the concern for what others think carried to a potentially destructive decision? In speaking directly with the boy about coming anyway, he candidly admitted he had too much to lose by disregarding his father's wishes. Who can say how much he will lose by giving in?

In organizational life the fear of what others think manifests itself in a variety of ways. One way is shown by people who want too much direction. A bank vice president in charge of operations wanted to know, "How do I keep my department heads out of my office?" He had found, upon taking his new job, that none of his department heads wanted to spell out what they themselves wanted to do. Rather, they all had the step-and-fetch-it syndrome of asking him to make every decision or to get his prior O.K.

before taking action. They were frightened of losing their positions if he was displeased. Little did they know that their over-dependent, oversensitive behavior was creating the very impression they were seeking to avoid; namely, that they didn't know what they were doing and couldn't be counted on to supervise their own areas.

This fear occurs when overpoliteness and formality are the rule within an organization. Because of the maintenance of formal relationships, the presentation of oneself through one's opinions and status can be carefully calculated to create a certain effect on others and to leave a predictable impression. Excessive energy is consumed to maintain facades in such formal organizations. In one large grocery chain, for example, everyone stood when the chairman of the board came into the room, as though he were a bishop, president, or supreme court justice.

More evidence of the effect of others' opinions upon most of us is the very importance we give to social norms. Behavioral scientists seek to change organizations by changing the social norms because they are aware of how sensitive people are to what others expect of them. The behavioral scientist in organizations doesn't seek to change individuals. He only has to change the unwritten rules of the organization, and people generally adapt, because people are more than ever oriented to social approval, especially by their associates.

Such social sensitivity makes people vulnerable to strictly utilitarian and exploitative values as well as to more human and people-centered values. The question is never, "Do we have a right to change norms?" Norms are manipulated by management constantly. The only question that we can ask is, "Change?—to what end?" Let it suffice here to point out that normative change rests on the socialization that has already taken place, which makes people not only susceptible to behavioral scientists but also to exploitative management, the media, advertising—even fads in speech and clothing. Socialization is also the basis for greater cooperation with others toward producing a more cohesive society. Such a goal holds value in our society. In many underdeveloped societies, no such cooperative value exists, which often puzzles the socialized American.

In discussing the effects of the fear of what others will think, often I have sounded negative. To some degree, that is a fair conclusion because most of us can become caught inextricably and unknowingly in social webs woven by friends, family, associates, and those we admire. Together, in their love and concern for us, they can overwhelm our own sense of what is right for ourselves at any given moment. They can, and most often will, quite unconsciously discourage risk on our part. In fact, I am so convinced of the destructive effects of some forms of love that I believe the progress of our entire nation can be attributed more to the collective energy of our society than to the popular myths of America's rugged individualism. Potential Paul Bunyan-like risk takers are most often rendered impotent by the protective love and dependence of their families.

The question may well be asked, "What can I do if from childhood I am conditioned to be responsive to the needs and wishes of others, often to the exclusion of my own needs?" First of all, you may be luckier than some. You may not be as susceptible to others' views and have as great a desire for peer recognition as some people have. Perhaps you can strike a good convergence between who you are and what others want you to be. The images are not always opposed. However, middle managers, as the middle class of management, often seem caught up in step-and-fetch-it attitudes. Like the department heads in the bank, you may think that checking every decision with the boss will keep you out of trouble. To second-guess what he wants you to be and do becomes your standard operating procedure, especially in hard times.

You may be right. Your boss may well be that kind of person. You must decide whether your job is worth the personal strength and integrity you will have to abandon in order to keep it. Like the kindergarten child, you will soon find you have fewer choices to make because the magic words will soon spew out automatically at your boss's cue. Many of you in that situation have developed such crippled egos that you could not even survive a change to a less socially constricted, less dependent organizational climate. For those of you still interested in cautiously taking chances, the latter half of the book will describe ways to practice being you. Sounds silly, doesn't it? The sad truth is that you may need practice. It has been so long.

FEAR OF UNCERTAINTY

You carry within yourself certain assumptions, expectations, and beliefs. These predispositions tend to control your judgment and behavior. They are the basis of stability, order, and sanity in an often fluid situation. To the extent that you, like Archie Bunker, are afraid to recognize new realities, you lose your ability to take creative risks and reap the joys as well as the sorrows of a passing age.

The history of the human race — economically, politically, religiously, socially, and scientifically — is emerging in a frightening, yet marvelous way. Those technologies, theories, and truths of today become the blocks which the builders of tomorrow reject. New technology, rapid urbanization, increased population, mobility, big business, bigger government, widespread affluence, decreased psychological size of this planet, and the horizons of a partly explored universe make "ancient good uncouth."

The greatest evidence of this developmental pace is demonstrated by the fact that when I first wrote these words in my doctoral thesis, I said, "horizons of an *unexplored* universe."

Can you take advantage of all of this progress? Archie Bunker holds certain truths to be self-evident that were generally acknowledged to be true a hundred years ago. Is this you? These include fixed views on minority groups, sex, work, education, religion, government, and country. Sound familiar? Archie has a nearly impossible time coping with new ideas, and usually deals with proposed changes by denying them, ridiculing them, or ignoring them. Part of his humor for us revolves around his reflection and mockery of some of our own beliefs. Archie is like middle management in his tenacity toward views that are no longer self-evident. He clings to what is known. He yells loudest when some idea challenges one of his own cherished assumptions. Ambiguity is not an acceptable concept to Archie. He has the correct opinion on every subject. He evidences a strong need to control people and ideas to prevent this dreaded ambiguity and uncertainty from fogging his view.

Like Archie, middle managers are often defending what *is* rather than what *is becoming*. In their anxiety to maintain the present, they lose perspective on the future, which is already with them and within them. They often consciously or unconsciously resist new procedures and resent major changes that executive management deems necessary in order to remain in business. Some of this fear may be part of the nature of the person, some may be generated on the job. Let's focus here on organizational factors.

Middle managers, often left uninformed about changes, make up their own explanations in order to appear reasonably intelligent to their employees. Perhaps being in the dark about the real future of the organization helps mold those reactionary attitudes of middle managers. An AMA report on managers says, "Today's manager reports that his opportunities for direct participation in the decision-making process seem to be rapidly decreasing in the highly bureaucratic and authoritarian structure of the technocorporation of the 1970s . . . for some, self-actualization seems entirely out of reach."[3] This conflicts with such expert observations as those of as astute a student of management as Thomas H. Patten, Jr.:

The old hierarchical system of authoritarian boss and compliant employee is already obsolete in many organizations. The only road to true efficiency seems to be that of persons communicating freely with persons through an individually initiated network which permits the flow of essential information throughout the organization. The bureaucratic form of organizations is increasingly becoming obsolete because it has been incapable of managing the tension between individual and managerial goals and the need to adapt to the scientific and technological revolution.[4]

I contend that Patten's statement is more the aspiration, but that the AMA survey is more the fact. The middle manager, left in ignorance and out of the decision-making circle, becomes more of an Archie Bunker and less of a risk taker. Not privy to the information and responsibility that bring on business and organization maturity, he often acts like the child he has been trained to be.

At this point I sound as if I have placed the major responsibility for the reactionary stance of middle managers on executive management. I have, although you must acknowledge a certain willingness on the part of most middle managers to be so treated (or they would demand a change). As organization children, they need not face the unknown, the uncertain, and the ambiguous, but can leave it all to the executive management: "That's what they get paid for, isn't it?" There is comfort and safety for middle managers in coping only with the known, and coping effectively.

You may recall the film or book *Bridge Over the River Kwai* by Pierre Boulle, which dramatizes the classic result of dealing only with the known to preserve certainty. You will remember that the colonel won his struggle for control of his own troops in the Japanese prison camp primarily because the Japanese colonel needed them to build a bridge which would permit the Japanese a whole new strategy in the war. The British colonel built the bridge within the time specified and made it a technical masterpiece. However, the British and Americans fighting the larger war saw the bridge and planned to destroy it. In the midst of their attempt to blow up the bridge, the British colonel sounded the alarm against the marauders because he could only grasp the fact that *his* bridge was about to be destroyed. He had lost all sight of the larger war. Not privy to the plans of his superiors, left only with the pride and power to do a job he knew how to do, he became a roadblock to the success of the greater effort. For this he was shot on the spot by one of the raiders representing his own executive management.

Without information and the initiative necessary to obtain it, middle managers are often obstacles to their own organization. In their fear of uncertainty, they often manufacture a spurious certainty. In their fear of the unknown, they may create information commonly called the grapevine, often distorted and inaccurate. With so little spelled out, they feel cautious and resistant. Certainly their fears inhibit risk taking.

This chapter has described three fears that motivate us and, when inordinate, distort our risk taking into foolish risks; or, as more often the case with middle managers, make them yield to cautious, careful, considered, controlled, and crafty decision making. These three fears are

Fear of failing. Fearing that their performance will be judged, some middle managers avoid situations such as management by objectives or changing jobs, even when they know intuitively that they are not seen as promising. I also suggested the subtler idea that many middle managers may really fear success. Success brings increased responsibility, greater potential for failure, and more independence when what middle managers may want above all else is to remain dependent. Failure is bad only for those who think it means they are bad, for those who introject, or for those who think it means that others are bad and who project. I emphasized that if you are caught in excessive fear of failing, only you can break the cycle and do something about it.

Fear of disapproval from others. Excessive preoccupation with others may cause you to act out bizarre image-creating activities or to become overcompliant and overly other-directed. I pointed out that American other-directedness has positive values in making a democracy work in a consensual manner. I also suggested that such other-directedness could be misused by connivers and could repress self-actualizing and creative risk taking. Middle managers may well be imbued with too much step-and-fetch-it for their own and their families' health, the effectiveness of their company, and the creativity of their nation.

Fear of uncertainty. This fear is common to us all. It drives us to keep some sanity and order in a rapidly changing world. However, if you are the Archie Bunker of middle management, you are reactionary to change. You are probably like the British colonel in *Bridge Over the River Kwai*. You focus on what you can control, rather than keeping an eye on the larger, uncertain situation. I also suggested that one organizational reason for middle management supercaution is that many middle managers aren't included often enough in the communication and decision-making process. However, rarely does middle management cry out indignantly at this kind of childish treatment. Instead, there is a kind of parent (executive management)–child (middle management) relationship that develops and is cherished and nourished by both.

4 | Do Groups Help or Hinder?

MORE THAN NINETY PERCENT of all managers would answer that question with a resounding "hinder." Everyone knows that groups are unadventurous and have a leveling effect. I, too, was raised on shibboleths such as, "the chain is no stronger than its weakest link," "a class is no faster than its dumbest student," and "a group is no riskier than its most conservative member." But it appears that the shibboleths are precisely that. Now, get this. There is no experimental evidence to support the assumption that groups have a conservative effect on the judgments of individuals. In fact, the numerous studies since 1961 on the effects of groups on risk taking allow investigators Clark and Willems to state categorically that, "The stability and replicability of the risky shift phenomenon are no longer questioned; the phenomenon can even be found in informal classroom demonstrations." [1] The phenomenon exists, and most research is now directed toward refining and choosing among interpretations of why the shift occurs.

THE RISKY SHIFT

The risky shift phenomenon can be defined in a variety of ways. For example, "When a group of people discuss a risk-taking problem, they usually arrive at a riskier solution than the

average of their own previous individual solutions."[2] "Using
risks and payoffs based on monetary gain and loss for problem-
solving performance, we observed that groups were considerably more likely than individuals to select the more difficult,
higher payoff (for correct solution) problems, even though problem solving was carried out by a single group member."[3] "The
common finding is that individuals are more willing to accept
risky decisions after participating in an interacting group than
they were willing to accept initially."[4] But you and I might reply,
"Certainly different conditions, subject matter, and people would
not permit such a statement to remain universally true." Not so!
In summary, the risky shift phenomenon states that groups influence individual decision making toward positions of higher
risk a significantly greater number of times than not, and under
almost any conditions.

Let's look at the several different experimental situations
where the risky shift has been observed. At the same time let's
see if some of our experience doesn't also support the experimental findings. I'll phrase the important questions as objections
and then answer them.

*The most dominant and risky people in the experimental
groups probably pressure the weaker ones.*

Not so! Whereas groups that interact show a greater risky shift,
people who simply listen to others on tapes and watch others
through one-way mirrors also shift toward greater risk when they
decide.

*People who make a decision under that kind of pressure
will still keep their private judgment as held before the
group meeting.*

Not so! Experiment after experiment has shown that individual
scores hold steady after the group risky shift took place, implying that individuals are really convinced, not simply high pres-
sured.

*These experiments were probably tried on some college
kids who were exceptionally open to being influenced.*

This also is not true. It is impressive that the risky shift phenomenon has been demonstrated in groups as small as three and as

large as fifteen. Differences in nationalities, ages, occupations, and sex have been included in the experiments with apparently no change in the risky shift phenomenon.

The experiments haven't taken place in the real world where risk involves one's own money or where even physical pain may result.

Again, untrue! Experimenters have shown that risky shift occurs even when the subjects are using their own money, although it is even more dramatic when using other people's money. Furthermore, risky shift occurs even when there are physically negative conditions that can result from larger versus smaller risks.

Perhaps the experimenters used subjects who were all biased the same way.

This could have been true at first, but not now. Experimenters have studied groups of people with highly divergent personal styles, personalities, and attributes. The phenomenon occurs in all groups with little variation. The only individuals not likely to shift are the ones already risky, not the conservative ones.

Experimentation continues. The reasons for the risky shift have yet to be explored. Related phenomena, such as the effect of risky leadership and its relation to perceived competence, also deserve attention. But that the shift does occur seems, beyond a doubt, to contradict many of the old wives' tales about the conservatism of group decisions. It would, in fact, be more reasonable for managers to beware lest groups consistently make risky choices simply because of the risky shift phenomenon and not because of the logic of the situation.

The concept of risky shift makes sense in light of our own experience, too. Why, for example, is there talk of middle manager unions? Because in a group middle managers will forge positions and demands that are riskier than most individual managers would take on their own. Here is one example of what happens when a supposedly happy set of middle managers is given the right to bargain. In Minnesota the legislature granted school principals the right to bargain with superintendents and school boards. In one district the principals denied having any interest in such a law. However, within ten days after the law's passing, a clandestine meeting was held by the principals which resulted in a representative organization with officers. The school superintendent felt betrayed.

In another example, a conference was held of 35 budget analysts in a state that decided to change from the divided program and budget format to an integrated one. Individually, many misgivings were expressed before the conference regarding the time frame to do the job, their ability to bring it off, whether the new 25 percent of the staff who were untrained could actually help, and the fear that the new state budget officer was taking them into uncharted waters that couldn't be sailed. Following the conference, during which people were openly encouraged to discuss pros and cons, there was universal support to "get to work." No stars existed in the old-timer's eyes, but their individual predictions as to outcome indicated a definite shift toward taking higher risks. Whether the collective judgment was more technically correct than the sum of the individual judgments prior to the conference can only be viewed from a time perspective sometime hence. But the risky shift phenomenon is clearly demonstrated here.

Other situations readily come to mind that, although dramatic, seem only to be bigger-than-life reenactments of everyday occurrences. We all remember the crowd in the cowboy show that hangs the innocent man; the boys on Halloween whose pranks are wilder than any one of them singly would have attempted; the company of marines that attempts the unreasonable; the minorities of women, blacks, and Indians who seek political and social equality; the mutual support, collusion, and self-delusion of the Watergate conspirators. All are examples of risky shift.

If groups do not insure the most conservative decision, neither do they consistently support the riskiest. This may, in fact, be the origin of the myth of the leveling effect of groups. Sometimes the need for risk is even greater than the group will admit. The entrepreneur will almost always want decisions that go beyond his employees' willingness to commit. The top manager may be looking for more imaginative responses from groups of cautious, uninformed middle managers who don't have the five-year picture and who are afraid to shoot for the moon and miss.

I think, then, we can say that when three or four are gathered together, we can count on a risky shift. The more times that top management involves middle management in face-to-face group decision making, the more risk taking these collective decisions will become, and middle managers will select the more difficult, higher payoff problems. Is that good? It depends upon the need within that corporation. For now, it is enough to change the fairy tale that groups make low risk decisions.

Before leaving the risky shift idea, I should point out that social scientists are trying to determine its cause. Two current hypotheses are ones you and I could have, and probably have, considered. The first is that risk taking, by implying boldness, may, in our society, be more socially desirable than conservatism. Most people think of themselves as no less risk taking than anyone else. When opinions are aired in a group, those of lesser risk bent tend to increase in risk taking, seeking to be seen as courageous rather than cowardly.[5] A second explanation is that as a result of the emotional bond developed between discussants, an individual feels less personal responsibility for failure of risking options than he would if deciding alone.[6] A third position is that of Dorwin Cartwright, who has questioned only recently the validity of the risky shift research design and the conclusions of 187 investigators from eight different countries since 1961.[7] Such criticism and disagreements are appropriate for social scientists. However, for the manager the evidence still stands that, indeed, under most circumstances, there will be a risky shift phenomenon.

So be it. The cause is of little interest to managers. They want to know about groups and what makes them tick. The risky shift is an important concept for them to consider in the groups in their organizations.

SHOULD YOU DEVELOP A TEAM?
THE RISKS AND TRADE-OFFS

First of all, let's talk about what teams and teamwork actually are. On one hand, we have Rensis Likert's linking groups of supervisors and supervisees. On the other, we have managers who talk about team building and teamwork as a spirit among employees. Is teamwork a reporting system, a formal structure, a particular group of people, or the old rah-rah? It is not clear whether we simply have a new catchword or one which, left undefined, can be used to include anything some management consultant wants to use to impress his client.

By my definition a corporate team is any group of three or more persons who have a common charter and an absolute need—not simply a desire—to cooperate in order to achieve the expected output. Such a group may be the corporation president and vice presidents, a department head and supervisors, a task force, an ad hoc committee, and so forth. To talk about teams when you are talking about the management of an organization where little interlocking activity actually takes place is simply talking euphemistically.

Don't mix up normal reporting structures with teams. It makes "team" a snicker word. It's like saying people are in love because they live together. A team needs a collective task that absolutely requires both technical and interpersonal coordination and emotional investment for success. Of course, any manager and those who report directly to him can improve their overall coordination and communication, but the word "team" should be carefully used for a special type of organization.

A good example of the problems around building teams was recently experienced by an assistant director of management for a large government agency. She had two men reporting to her. One was the head of personnel; the other directed the smaller, more elite group of management analysts. Her personal agenda upon becoming their supervisor was to make the two divisions into a more interdependent team. She wanted them to work together on establishing zero-based manpower plans and creating long-range manpower development programs to be integrated into the agency's long-range program and budget. After several false starts, she finally, wisely, gave up the team concept, even though it was dear to her heart.

One might say perhaps it was their personalities that prevented them from investing in the concept of a single organization. Perhaps, but I think not. Rather, there was no necessity for great interdivisional relationships. All such an organization could do was to shift the energy already being applied to individual missions to the task of working out an abstractly better, closer integration. They performed two separate functions. Becoming anything more than supportive of each other was not desirable.

In another case even the apparent singleness of mission wasn't enough to create a team. The owner of a small excavation firm wanted to replace his resigned executive vice president with a management team. After carefully selecting a team made up of the top engineer, the business manager, the head of the truck drivers, and the top bulldozer foreman, he gave them a year and a great deal of outside consulting assistance to build a responsible team. During this period he also initiated a stock purchase plan that would give them the opportunity to own the company. However, the foreman never understood why he should learn about business problems. He even refused to go on salary. The engineer always worried about what the owner might want. The head of the truckers really didn't like meetings, and only the business manager seemed interested in the larger concerns of management. In other words, even though they were selected carefully, these people could not grasp the need to become a team in order to fulfill the responsibility they had been given. The result was a poorly developed team with little real mutual help and cooperation. The owner rehired the executive vice president and fired the consultants.

Let's assume that your organization meets the two criteria of singleness of mission and absolute need to cooperate. I suggest further that the nature of the individuals themselves is important to consider. Are they team players? You must look at your group and decide whether there are too many loners who are uncomfortable and unskilled at working in groups to ever make the transition.

Even with a common mission team building is not easy. People's motivations are different. Some are ambitious, devious, uncooperative; others are abrasive, self-seeking, complacent. Still others are afraid of the responsibility success brings; many just feel incompetent in groups. How much do people have to like each other? How much do they have to respect each other? How close do they have to become? How much leadership must each exert? How can normal needs that depend on associates be met without jeopardizing one's status of equality? The questions go on and on. Only a particular team can answer these questions as pertains to its way of working together.

Then you must examine your organizational climate. How autonomous are you? Can your boss stop you from building a team whenever he wishes? Can you get financial support for team-building training activities? Will your colleagues simply see you as attempting to best them with a new gimmick? These and other questions will have to be answered before you can feel free to take you and your associates into a genuine period of team building.

At this point, while you are assessing your situation and answering these questions, let's talk about the potential value of teams. In a later chapter I'll suggest a dramatic corporate model of teams, but for now we will concentrate on why teams help more than hinder and what the risks are to the manager who builds a team rather than uses one-to-one management techniques. Again, let's use the objection approach. Standard objections almost always have some basis in truth, which is why they are appealing. They need to be confronted directly if they are to be delved for whatever truth they hold.

First, let's deal with some objections that you as a manager may have:

If I develop a team I'll have less personal control. I'll be more subject to group decisions and not be as effective a manager. Where does group authority over me start and stop?

Of course, you are right! Ground rules on decision making must be clear, and you will often have to hang in tough. More conflict will be demanded and from time to time you will be attacked. But, remember, you will be gaining a new collective energy that will be used to solve problems creatively, not just to control you. In the final analysis, most people want a boss, manager, leader, or whatever. The biggest difference for you would be learning to work more with a group than just with individuals on a one-to-one basis. Most managers lack those skills. They've operated for years on the concept of divide and conquer.

If I share my management functions with the team, too many things will fall between the cracks.

Quite possibly, at first. But after a reasonable period of time and some team-building training, self-discipline and group discipline will evolve. When someone drops the ball you won't be the only screamer. A true team effort means that your end affects mine. Individual performance records become team property.

We don't have time to meet in groups as much as this team business would require. I know some organizations that simply live in groups and hardly get their work done.

There is no question that teams do require more time in meeting as groups or subgroups. Emphasis is put on achieving the best possible communication, not only in objective ways such as memos but in subjective face-to-face ways that only occur when people get together. Also, at the beginning of learning to work as a team, more time is needed, most often because many individuals feel that their self-interests or concerns will not be adequately represented by anyone else on the team.

Ideally, however, like a good marriage or friendship, people come to believe that the other people care about their concerns and themselves as well. Second, they learn to predict each other's response to any given problem so that they can actually represent each other's point of view. This trust of each other's predictability finally permits a team to have group meetings only when that's the only way to get a particular task done, or when policy or personnel matters must be dealt with.

If I start a team, I'll become more personally vulnerable to open criticism.

That's true, but not necessarily bad, because many managers don't get adequate feedback. It is not good if the team uses you for the scapegoat, but such a situation would be highly unlikely. They, more often, would select a weaker member of the team to admonish inappropriately. You will be busier protecting that person than yourself.

It is true that an effective team learns to occasionally examine its own decision-making processes and, in general, its ability to work together. To this extent you'll have to share feelings about the group and individuals in a group setting. Such a procedure may be strange to you. You may feel somewhat exposed at first, but with time it becomes a tool of the group's own management effectiveness. Good managers know that nothing leads to poorer management than unexamined management practices.

Other objections to teams may come from your subordinates themselves. They may be quite similar to yours. The following are ones I've heard from employees:

Why should I be responsible to a team rather than to just the boss? They'll try to run my life.

To some degree just as you share your management control with your associates, they also begin having more than one boss — not other individuals but a team. They may feel a loss of freedom but most will also feel a gain in support, understanding, and effective help.

Why should I take on increased responsibility of teamwork without more pay?

This is difficult to answer, especially for those who don't like groups to begin with. However, if properly planned, teams can be compensated in such a way as to override that objection. In most cases, the new influence the employee will gain as part of the output of the entire team will more than compensate for the apparent demand for increased involvement with colleagues brought on by building a team.

I don't like to manage. Furthermore, we use my creative time and I resent it.

This is a telling argument against building a team, and could prevent a team from forming. Some adjustments may have to be made for a particular kind of group. On the other hand, unless you are part of an R&D group that has little accountability, no one should be allowed not to worry about cost benefit problems. Is management only the job of some particular class of people? Even my 15-year-old son is held accountable for management concerns in my home. Should an employee have less responsibility? Only you, in your unique situation, can answer the question.

The following summarizes the potential losses and gains of building a team, looked at in the worst and best possible lights:

Potential Losses	Potential Gains
Less management control	More employee self-discipline and control
Manager's authority becomes less clear	Group takes more risks and assumes more responsibility
Individual follow-through jeopardized when responsibility is joint	More willingness to pick up each other's dropped balls
Too much time spent in groups	Better communication and synergy of effort
Everyone more vulnerable to criticism	Greater personal and professional growth
Time and creative energy spent on management concerns	More accurate information and overview provided on current situations for all

CHECK YOUR OWN ATTITUDES

The final test of whether you can lead a team effort or even be a significant part of a team is when you actually try it. I once had a young man who was a part of my own organization who was ideologically the purest team man I've ever encountered. We kidded him about being the resident idealist and dogmatician. However, in actual experience in his job as business manager, he consistently acted in noncollaborative ways. He made decisions for people and for the company without following ground rules, and often he procrastinated in carrying out instructions. Mind you, I still believe to this day that his behavior had been learned in organizations where trust was low and collaboration anathema. His head and heart were committed to participation and teamwork, but his feet trod a different path. The same may be true of you.

Here are some basic attitudes that effective team leaders

seem to have. I have drawn them from the excellent work of Sven Lundstedt of the Ohio State University.[8] Of course, every team manager doesn't possess all these attitudes, but to distribute power and get the maximum from the team, many of these attributes are necessary. Check yourself for your ability to take these risks in leading a team.

- —I can give freedom and responsibility to others without knowing them very well.
- —As a rule I don't have to watch and control people to be a good supervisor.
- —I can trust people with influence and responsibility when I'm not around.
- —Obviously each individual is to be considered differently, but people generally come through if you give them a chance.
- —I'll stick out my neck to delegate even though I've been burned many times.
- —I find that people have a great deal of talent and energy that can only be developed by giving them lots of room to express it.
- —I try to delegate freely because you never know when you'll find hidden talents in your organization.
- —I often take long shots on people.
- —I have a gambling spirit and a faith in the future, even though I rarely know what it holds.
- —I think a good executive takes risks, especially on people.

Now that you've rated yourself, try to predict how your boss and your boss's boss would answer. When you build a team, remember the owner can get a new manager. Don't think a company that generally opposes those values will value you and your teams. Be a creative, moderate risk taker, not a fool.

In this chapter we examined three major concepts. We looked at groups and their effect on decisions, we looked at teams and their effect on middle managers, and we looked at our attitudes toward both.

The most significant effect that groups have on the decision-making process is defined by the concept of the risky shift. The risky shift phenomenon states that groups influence individual decision making toward positions of higher risk more often than not and under almost any conditions. Studies in this area shatter any theory that says groups have a leveling influence on decision making.

Groups in the working world can be built into teams. A team can only exist where there are three or more people who have a common charter and an absolute need to cooperate to achieve the expected result. If these criteria are met and you have some good team players, you can develop a corporate team. The question is, "Should you?" The decision is yours.

Finally, the concept of the team players was enlarged. The necessary attributes of the team player and the team leader were given for you to examine yourself and the corporate atmosphere in which you work.

UNIT TWO
THE MEDIOCRITY
OF MIDDLE
MANAGEMENT

THE PROVOCATIVE TITLE of this unit is meant to challenge middle managers to assess their performance as a management class. It is important for them to understand what the corporate environment is for middle managers and how they react to it. Chapter 5 describes the frustrations of middle management but with, it must be confessed, little accounting for what currently makes them happy. I assume something has made them satisfied in the past, but Chapter 5 shows how the trend is toward disenchantment rather than satisfaction.

To what degree, then, are these frustrations subject to influence by middle managers themselves? Well, first of all, they have to see that they can't remain complacent. To further explore this fact, Chapter 6 points out the risk of not risking. Then Chapter 7 suggests that in order to discover the energy within themselves to change the situation, middle managers must have, or must develop, a rigorous belief system—a set of values or philosophy of life—to guide them.

Finally, in Chapter 8 middle managers can examine themselves in the nexus of the two factors of risk taking and creativity and begin to set their goals.

5 | Ignored, Not Despised

AN AMA SEMINAR was held to discuss a fascinating research report on manager unions.[1] The survey results confirmed much of my own experience, that middle manager frustration is indeed on the rise. There are some threats of unionization among middle management groups, and top management is probably going to ignore the whole thing. The seminar itself was evidence of the lack of interest from the top. The seminar was billed for top management, but not one president of any company, health organization, or volunteer organization or any top government or church official attended. One presenter, A. G. Barry, was greatly upset by the lack of top management participation. I was not surprised. Top management's absence was but a symptom of the real frustration of middle management, that is, being the "forgotten people of management."[2] In what ways are they forgotten?

Out of the loop. First of all, middle managers are left out of the loop. That is, they are rarely in on company decision making; most often, they are not told what's happening or why. Managers may be assigned to a new department or to a new town with hardly a by-your-leave. They may think that someone is intentionally moving them out of spite or trying to force them to leave the company. But the truth is that their feelings, family, and career goals may not have been discussed at all, depending on

61

their management level or the particular company's policies in the matter. They are not discriminated against. They aren't even remembered. According to the AMA survey,

Today's manager is deeply concerned about what he regards as an increasing tendency toward greater responsibility without a corresponding increase in authority. Today's manager reports that his opportunities for direct participation in the decision-making process seem to be rapidly decreasing in the highly bureaucratic and authoritarian structure of the techno-corporation of the 1970s.[3]

Underutilization. Frustration at being out of the loop has many consequences for middle managers and the companies for which they work. Most middle managers can't figure out why top management wants people with expensive educations, much on-the-job experience, and continued management training in decision making, when, at the same time, these same people seem to be less appreciated, less respected, given less recognition for what they accomplish, and increasingly are given step-and-fetch-it functions to perform. Top management's attitude is very similar to the rich person who wants one of the best of everything, even though it's used only once a year.

Executives blind to the people in middle management often are unaware of the strengths and abilities of this group. In one company top management was encouraged to ask middle managers to recommend alternatives for an electronics line that consistently lost money. The middle managers spent tremendous energy, demonstrated a depth of unrecognized business understanding, and exhibited objectivity even when an alternative affected their jobs negatively—much to the astonishment of top management. Such cases rarely happen because middle management seldom *demands* more authority and therefore is never recognized for its extensive talents.

Left in the dust. Middle managers are forgotten when it comes to money, security, fringe benefits, and advancement. They are most concerned that the "gains secured by blue collar unions (are) outpacing gains of management employees." They see their salaries as low or with many negatives. The recession in the 1960s convinced them that they should be concerned about their long-term security, and great numbers are opting for that, rather than for personal reward and achievement. All of these problems and frustrations are those of people no longer (if ever they were) seen as either a force to be dealt with, such as blue collar unions, or a group to be coddled.

Pawns in the game. Of course, top management can always say, "Who's concerned about us?" Presidents often feel hemmed in by the chairman's personal needs for an apartment in Spain or a yacht in Florida. Sometimes in a one-owner company, the owner will place impossible demands, such as, "Give my son or daughter a good job," even though he or she is incompetent. One company president had the owner's son in charge of the foreign subsidiaries. The son, wearing a cowboy suit, would frequent both Japan and Holland more than the subsidiaries could take; but it did get him out of the country.

Middle managers, when seeing top management as their nemesis, often do not appreciate that the president or vice president may well be the victim rather than the architect of management problems. "The power politics of the executive suite sometimes limit his ability to act in meaningful and dramatic ways." If the top man is bound, how much more the middle manager? For example, if the president attempts to bring middle management into the loop, he increases his vulnerability to criticism, so that any downturn in company progress may be seen as "soft" management by the board. The president has the problem that, "If he pushes too hard for change, or makes arbitrary changes which are out of the mainstream, he will find himself out of a job." Therefore, he is concerned with his own survival and that of the company. Because of these forces on the complex manning of the modern corporation, middle managers often become pawns, bishops, and knights.

TAKE THE SITUATION IN HAND

How do blue collar workers get more attention? By militantly squeaking until they're greased! They don't expect top management to spend long hours benevolently worrying about them. They look at the balance sheet and demand their due. Management then deals with them, often gratefully. I say "gratefully," because top management prefers to deal with a progressive company-oriented (as well as worker-oriented) union. Workers acting in unison mean less worry for management about inequities of salary, grievances, troublemakers, and other labor problems of the past. Once the contract is signed, management can demand the worker's full attention to the task. There are drawbacks to unions, but most top managements today would probably not give them up if the option arose.

Thus middle managers are ignored by being left out of the decision and information loop and treated neither as top management's serious adversary, such as blue collar workers, nor favored with the extras of being friends of top management. While top management continues to ignore you and treat you like trusted mammys to run their households, you are becoming obsolete. Youngsters come into the firm who are bright and have new approaches with which you aren't familiar. Because of your role—which has been to maintain the old rather than innovate the new—organizational shifts, mergers, acquisitions, and company policy changes make you nervous—perhaps, rightly so. You never know (and that's a key point) when one of those eternal shuffles will land you out the door. Even though pay and fringes may not be bad, you know that your paycheck reflects smaller annual increases every year, which could be taken as a sign of your decreasing value to top management.[4]

Most of you, then, are in a trap, partially of your own making. As top management's stewards, you make enough so that you can't quit and go back to school at 35 because your children are too young. Once you pass 40, you feel you can't compete with younger people in a new profession. Few companies today are willing to pay for that career transition, even though they often talk about it.

Middle managers still expect the corporation to "care." A college in Tennessee has a motto, "The college that cares." The implication is that this institution acts in some continually concerned way about its students. I never met an institution face to face, much less seen one that "cares."

One sales manager who worked for an aluminum company epitomizes the middle manager who thought the company cared. After some initial success in the company's sales force he was given 25 salesmen to supervise. Then over the next 10 years the territory was reorganized three times. Each time he lost people reporting to him. At the end of the ten years, when he talked to me, he had lost all his subordinates. He was making a little more money, but had more territory to cover. He was 45 years old and couldn't understand what was happening to him.

I encouraged a confrontation with top management, which, on reflection, may not have been useful, or a career change. He had contacts. He could be a rep. He could do what he was doing then, but do it for himself, not for the company, which, obviously, was giving him a message. But, no. Somehow he still felt that the company cared. He wanted to depend on some omnipotent force that would keep its eye on him like God does on the sparrow. He personalized the company, even though it was a large, complex bureaucracy whose minions had passed over him several times at promotion periods. The company didn't care. No company cares.

You aren't hated. You are the forgotten person in management. The pick of the crop has gone "up." This particular middle manager may not consider leaving the company or forming a union, but many are, especially the 20 to 29 year olds. It is possible, even now: Under existing NLRB rulings those managers who do not actually supervise workers are allowed to organize.[5] It may be the only way they can get the attention of top management. But to do so will involve risks that apparently they aren't yet willing or able to take. Middle managers, even though left out of the loop, still think the company cares—a comforting but unrealistic delusion.

MINORITY MANAGEMENT DISABILITIES

I've included whites, blacks and other minorities, as well as women and men in the former discussion. However, women and minorities have added disabilities. Those in middle management are likely never or rarely to change chairs when the next reorganization takes place except, perhaps, into some other staff position. Blacks in white collar jobs experience greater discrimination (29 percent) than blacks in blue collar jobs (12 percent).[6] Blacks find they must make more money to live at white levels because the minority dollar buys less. Ten grand doesn't buy the same amount of housing, education, or consumer goods for them.

In a government agency, a black man was selected to administer an equal opportunity compliance program. Generally, the blacks felt he was an Oreo cookie—white on the inside and black on the outside. Both black and white women felt he was a male chauvinist, and when he wanted a female rather than a male assistant, saw this as confirmation of their views of him. His white top management had picked him for his known moderate views, but then was frustrated by his apparent inability to get things done. To the top man, this meant installing a system of reporting numerical compliance with affirmative action plans as established by the whole company. To others, it meant that certain employers were still screwing the system and not really trying to bring in minorities. In every case the man could do no right. It is not fashionable in the 1970s for a black to appear to be close to whites or to advocate integration. On the other hand, as long as he ". . . looks like, thinks like, acts like his racial minority reference group, he or she will never become a legitimate member or leader of the United States racial majority." [7]

How about the upward mobility of black middle managers? If they perform poorly they will almost never be demoted. They will be moved laterally into a staff job with no one to report to them. As far as "up" is concerned, the evidence is pretty clear that "up" is not very high in the hierarchy. Today

There are no senior blacks at the top of any major American corporation, nor are there any blacks at the senior level (dean or full professor) at any of the major business schools.

There are men of color willing and able to manage senior divisions of *Fortune* 500 companies, yet not one has had the opportunity. For decades scores of these historically disadvantaged graduates had had Ph.D.s and D.B.A.s and yet not one has reached the level of full professor at the leading professional schools of business. [8]

The limitations on blacks for upward mobility seem almost infinite, not because of lack of talent but because of color. With the decrease of overt black unrest, top management once again has settled into its doldrums of coping practically with its worst problems, and apparently white collar blacks are beginning to think like their white counterparts, that the company cares.

While certainly true of minorities of any kind, it is especially true for women that a major barrier to their full utilization in the workforce is the result of the promulgation of myths and generalizations about women as a group. Most of these can be easily countered with intellectual arguments and statistics, but women who have become middle managers know that in reality such myths are almost impossible to overcome. Let's examine some of the more work-related male assumptions and why they frustrate women who want responsibility, comradeship, and upward mobility.

Women get married and have children, leading to excessive absenteeism and high turnover rate.

According to national statistics, of the female workforce, which was 31.5 million in 1970, four out of ten women were mothers.[9] Of these four, only 36 percent have children under the age of six. A U.S. Public Health Service survey of work time lost due to illness or injury revealed that women lost, on the average, 5.6 days as compared to 5.3 for men. Maybe the reader's experience is different. Maybe your experience or statistics reflects higher turnover rates or absenteeism. Perhaps, then, you should reexamine the kinds of jobs that make up your sample.

In point of fact, most of the 31.5 million women are restricted to clerical and other low-status jobs. Shorter tenure and relatively lower commitment may be linked with women employed in jobs with little prospect for advancement or job satisfaction. There are factories, job shops, and manufacturing organizations by the dozens where women are the workers and foremen are indeed *foremen.* This general subjugation prevents women from aspiring to higher positions.

Women middle managers experience the frustrations of being treated as if they were less ambitious and committed than their male counterparts, and "if they aren't, they should be." Generally, men lump all women into the category of working only to help their husbands, not because they want careers. Therefore they are expected to have less ambition and take less pay. This is, in fact, a subtle way for a male oligarchy to reinforce the concept that men are the true breadwinners, because when the husband makes less than his wife, there is still a cultural suspicion that he's no good. Ironically, if there were less sex bias in business, the

man's income might more often be marginal, and the self-supporting women, female family heads, and the families dependent on
the wife's earnings would be more the norm and women more
secure. But women are seen as secondary income producers and,
as a result, their earnings do not increase as they gain additional
experience. Thus the male-female earnings gap widens with age.

*Women should be unaggressive, noncompetitive, and,
if self-confident, unassuming.*

The problems this creates for women interested in management
are profound. To hold administrative office aggression, self-confidence, and competitive drive must be exhibited, and women
who show these necessary traits violate cultural roles and cause
embarrassment and anxiety in the men (and often, women) with
whom they work. Therefore they are reluctant to pursue upward
mobility.[10] In a day when managers' abilities to present themselves are often more important than principles or integrity,
women are at a disadvantage. Their presentations must be
feminine or they will not be accepted; conversely, if they are
feminine, they will not be seen as tough enough for the job—a
neat double bind for the female middle managers. In other words,
if they meet expectations, they will be seen as inadequate by male
standards. If they don't meet expectations for females, they will
be feared as masculine or castrating.

No one likes to work for a woman supervisor.

"A Department of Labor survey indicates that at least three-
fourths of both male and female respond ents [all executives] who
had worked for women held favorable views of women supervisors."[11] When such a myth, however, is generally held to be
true, it appears in the boardroom and in the executive suites when
the time comes to choose a new vice president. There are
notable exceptions where women are vice presidents in small
firms with which they have been associated from their inception.
But, in general, there is no all-out program in business to develop
female managers. The result is that career women are hard
pressed to move up the ladder of management.

For example, some years ago I offered a consultant position to
a very competent young woman in the training department of a
large corporation that developed control systems. She refused to

join me because she wanted management rather than consulting and therefore desired to remain with the company for which she then worked. A year later she left that company and joined a small manufacturing firm to be a manager of people development. She had no one reporting to her and her new bosses hardly knew what the concept of management was. A challenging situation? Maybe. But had she been a male, given the talents she had, her star would have risen in her former organization. There is no doubt in my mind. That is what frustrates women.

Certain jobs are male and certain jobs are female.

Most of us (over 30) find it difficult not to do sex typing. I don't like my wife to carry the portable TV upstairs. That's man's work. She likes me to wash the car. That's man's work. I like her to wrap the Christmas packages and make social engagements. That's women's work. These sexist thoughts are also projected into the marketplace. Those jobs associated with nurturing and homemaking seem appropriate for women. These include nursing, teaching, personnel work, counselors, social workers, secretaries, airline hostesses, and telephone operators. As an example of violated expectations, I'm still taken aback when I call information and a man answers.

Men, on the other hand, extrapolate from the characteristics of home responsibilities to become plumbers, doctors, engineers, school administrators, managers, and bank presidents. These are, for the most part, not people-helping jobs. One male company president says: "There are two kinds of people: thing-people and people-people. Women tend to be lumped into the people-people jobs and men into the thing-people jobs."

The situations created by these biases hurt the opportunities of men as well as women, because there are people-people and thing-people in both sexes. Male secretaries are still expected to be effeminate and female production managers to be masculine, if not lesbian. Of course, sex labeling is not new, and the picture is changing. The problem is that the divisions of work break down quicker into lower-status, lower-paying jobs such as school crossing guards, paperboys, stewardesses, and church acolytes. Middle and top management tend to be the province of white males, and the myths we cited about women are particularly those that affect female mobility.

If women in general suffer from prejudice, special venom is reserved for the solo woman in management. She is stereotyped as either a sexual attraction or distraction. Middle and top management's wives want to know when she is going with their husbands on a business trip—"Who else is going?" Fellow workers discuss her looks and ignore her competence in ways they would never apply to a male. She often feels alone, exploited, and demeaned. She tends to be the secretary of any committee on which she serves. Her complaints usually fall on deaf ears or are seen as special pleading. Men, adding to the problem, seem prone to compete for her attentions, which she neither wants nor needs.

Many companies, rather than having to cope with these problems, will simply eliminate the problem by keeping women, especially single ones, out of middle and certainly out of top management. In so doing, one source of company stress is removed, and, from my point of view, a great deal of talent is underutilized. The barrier is great; the solution as yet unclear. The talented, management-oriented career woman is at a distinct disadvantage. The cultural problems are real and present. Top management tends to cope only with what it must. It will ignore this one as long as possible.

One special group must be noted as perhaps being at the bottom of the pile when it comes to upward mobility in business: the minority female. The minority female is the enemy of everyone who wants to get ahead. She, especially if attractive and intelligent, is vying for the job the black (or Indian or Chicano) male might be able to get. And she has all the disabilities of the white woman. Other women will fear her, see her as possibly getting breaks they can't because of her race. The white male manager will almost always see her through minority as well as sexist stereotypes. He may be far less threatened by her, but he wouldn't want to work for her. So there she is—a super solo person with enemies at all corners of the table. Black women who succeed in management are a special breed and should receive the Order of Personal Survival Against All Odds.

This chapter points out that all people—male and female, majority and minority—have special frustrations. Some are caused by the people themselves; some are caused by forces beyond anyone's direct control. But others are inexcusable, and middle managers can do something about them.

You, as a member of a minority group, whether racial or sexual or both, have additional frustrations. Your upward mobility will be controlled by the conscious and unconscious racism and sexism of our culture. In most cases you are not a serious threat to top management because they tend to be fire-fighters. Why should top executives waste their time and energy on minorities in management when there aren't enough to cause trouble? Top management is hardly concerned that you will squeak for more grease. You are all too few. You are judged by stereotypes too numerous and unfounded to mention. The answers for you may not be found without a major cultural and corporate renewal.

Finally, even middle managers would agree that there is little threat from women. In the AMA report *Manager Unions?*, of the 19 conditions rated by middle managers as most likely to produce middle management frustration and discontent with and alienation from top management, the one at the bottom of every list was "substantial influx of women into top management positions." One could interpret this by saying that middle managers wouldn't mind working for women in top management. A more realistic view is that they saw, neither now nor in the future, no likelihood of that happening.

I've pointed out that, in general, there are no large organizations that care. Individuals may care but not companies. Middle managers are out of the decision and information loop. They are not given proper care for their economic security, nor are they properly retrained and redirected when upward mobility no longer seems possible.

What can *you* do? How long has it been since you made a demand of any sort to top management? Does it remember who you are and does it appreciate the fact that you are minding the store? You may be slowly stagnating, becoming less and less the dynamic manager it hired. You may expect the company to be concerned about your corporate fate, but that is a dream. You might consider unionizing. You may have to band together to make enough noise to be heard.

6 | The Risk of Not Risking

PERHAPS THE BEST REASON for becoming a creative risk taker is summed up in a biblical quote from Mark that refers to the reward of the righteous: "For he that hath, to him shall be given; and he that hath not, from him shall be taken away even that which he hath." Broadly applied, this phrase is the substance of why one should risk. It suggests that if you don't risk loving, you lose the capacity to love. If you don't think big, you lose the capacity to think big. If you don't try the untried, soon the untried becomes frightening and mysterious. On the other hand, those who love gain greater ability to love. What is true emotionally is true physiologically. If one lies in bed for extended periods and doesn't use one's limbs, the ability to use them at all is curtailed. If the senses aren't challenged they lose their acuity.

This chapter contends that if you don't take risks you lose your capacity to do so. That is the risk of not risking. Those who think big soon find thinking bigger to be a habit. Those who venture soon find new strengths and skills with which to venture. Truly, the spiritual or economically rich person gets richer and the spiritual or economically poor gets poorer. The truism may not be popular but life seems to sustain the reality of it.

Knowing, then, that if you don't risk you lose part of your capacity to do anything, let's look at how risk taking helps you to make money, build relationships, and fully realize your potential.

MAKING MONEY

We all know you have to risk to make money. We also know that so long as you work for money rather than money working for you, you won't make money. To make money, then, you need money. You must either have money of your own or use somebody else's. But to get more, you must have some.

One man I know took a series of calculated risks which made him a millionaire. He and a friend started with a small insurance brokerage firm in the midwest. The firm was relatively successful, but he found the profit margins being squeezed by the underwriters, and the working hours becoming longer. He and his partner agreed to broaden their income base. They decided to build a building and rent out part of it to other businesses. They located a landowner who didn't want to sell his land because of capital gains problems, but who would lease them property on easy payments. They leased the property in a relatively underdeveloped area that had promise. Then they borrowed money from a local bank. Their collateral was the leased land and their personal notes and 80 percent occupancy guarantee for the building. Getting the loan was not easy, even though they were hometown kids.

They had hardly put up the building when it was full of new tenants. As a result of their earlier reflection on the nature of insurance brokering, they sold their agency. Then, with that collateral, they went to the bank; again, using leased land and their newly sold business, they put up a six-story office building next to the smaller one they had already built. The bank was more generous this time, only requiring that they guarantee 50 percent occupancy before the first shovel touch d the dirt. They were able to get 70 percent, and before the building was actually put up, they had 100 percent occupancy.

From these successes they continued expanding, leasing more land and building more buildings, until an insurance company bought into the firm by paying several millions of dollars in cash and stock to my friends to enable them to gain controlling interest. Only five years had passed! Today, he and his associate still run the operation and are yet expanding in other directions.

In describing his success, my friend said that when he had

little the banks were difficult to borrow from. He had had to demonstrate liquidity, take a high interest rate, and hold his hat in his hand to get his first loans. Three years later they were giving him more than perhaps they should have, charging him lower interest rates, and coming to his office. To him who has will more be given. To get money means to take creative risks.

One effect of not making money is forgetting how to do it. There is a reason that the poor of the United States are often poor generation after generation. It isn't that they are retarded. It isn't even a lack of capital. No, they have lost the drive to achieve, which results in forgetting how. Of course, the converse is also true. If you learn how to make money, it's hard to stop. Quite unconsciously, you do the things that make money. That's why the rich get richer and the poor get poorer. Rich people get richer not only because they have capital but because they know what to do with it and often enjoy doing it.

Why Take a Chance?

Middle managers often have full stomachs, although there is uncertainty regarding future needs. They say, "But why take risk? I've got enough to live on. I have a pension plan in which I'm partly vested (even though it is nontransferable). I have medical plans, social security, and I put a little away. Isn't that enough?" Maybe not; for some, maybe. But if all of us thought it possible, wouldn't we want more? Isn't it human to want more, to acquire, or to spend?

I see three kinds of people as far as money is concerned. Those who never developed or lost their capacity (denialists), those who make money and spend it (materialists), and those who like to pile it up (capitalists). People who know how to make money seldom reject the making of it. By definition, they make it. Let's assume that you are of the first class—the denialist—which is where most middle managers could be assigned. If so, you may have lost the capacity or never learned how to make money, but let's presume the pilot light is on even if the fire is out. Why should you take any risks if you have received the benefits of corporate life?

If you rest on your laurels, you may lose your job at 50. What company sees itself as a rest farm for middle-aged has-beens? In fact, you may be losing the very motivation and values that attracted the company to you in the first place, quite without knowing it. While I'm not suggesting that you should only be pursuing money, I am saying that money, not security programs, company golf courses, company-sponsored trips, company golf club memberships, and the like, is something you had better not risk forgetting how to acquire. If you find yourself on the street at 50, you'll have to figure out how to get money, maybe a job. You're bound to go looking for advice. "How do I start?" you'll ask. I've never had a manager ask me how to get a job to whom I didn't say, "Forget it. Your goal is wrong. Figure out what you have that other people want, and sell it to them."

I particularly remember a man in personnel, out of his third low-paying middle manager job after ten years. He loved to do the church books as the treasurer. I told him that was a great business. Lots of churches would like his services. A few sets of church books and he was on easy street, setting his own hours and pay. My intent wasn't to drive him out of the corporate world. The corporate world needs able people. But I felt that one reason he had been fired related to his stodginess, low risk taking, and lack of initiative. If he couldn't please a company, I thought, perhaps he could please himself. He should have been taught as a child, as we all should teach our children, how to make money so that they can have survival skills when they need them, now or at 50.

You may become very bored with all that security. Instead of using your energy toward achieving, you may use lovers, alcohol, downers, and uppers to screw up your life. Indeed, if middle managers are frustrated in trying to be involved, get recognized, get paid, be upwardly mobile, be retrained, then their energies have to go somewhere. If 12- to 18-year-olds, bored by an unchallenging, uncaring world, take dope, what are the parents doing? Are they taking uppers, downers, alcohol, preludin, or other narcotics because they, too, are bored? The TV says, "Where are you children tonight?" Maybe someone should be saying, "Where are your parents tonight?" Having an affair with a colleague's spouse, taking dope, joining swingers' clubs, and sitting in hard-core porno movies are no substitutes for making money, and they are far riskier.

Money is just fun to have. Better to get it and then demonstrate that you are the world's greatest humanitarian, spendthrift, or hoarder. Money does things you want done. If it is used inappropriately, then that's a human problem; but money, like education, is simply the tool which can serve any master.

Money gives personal freedom. All wives and husbands should have enough money so that they can be sure they stay together because they want to, not because they have to. When you have money you can sleep on the beach or in the tenth-floor suite. You can live in a shack or buy in Larchmont. You can live high in America or start an African medical hospital. The point is that money gives you freedom to choose. Poverty is no choice as long as you are poor.

Religious people for years have said, "It is easier for a camel to pass through the eye of a needle than for a rich man to enter the kingdom of heaven." This has been interpreted to mean that one shouldn't make money. I feel that this is not truly the Christian attitude toward making money. Such an interpretation could only be that of people avoiding difficulty, and having money is difficult. It does give you more choices. One is tempted to misuse and abuse it. But money and the making of it aren't bad. They are an appropriate outlet for our creative energies. It's fun!

Money making shifts your focus from merely holding a job to producing something of merit. The Department of Labor put out a handbook for youngsters several years ago suggesting that since there were no jobs available, they might need help, so here were some ways to make money — *to make money!* Find a service to perform, wash a window, a car, a dog. Paint garbage cans. Make something and sell it. Tell me what has happened in America when the government has to publish a book telling our children how to make money because they are looking for jobs that don't exist. We are, by example, teaching our kids that the economic aim of life is to get a job rather than to make money. It's outrageous that they have never learned the feeling of being able to make money. Perhaps that's why, when a youngster approaches me on the 10th hole, his pocket full of balls to sell, I always, always buy. He may be a dying breed. He is interested in making money. He'll soon be taking risks for even bigger stakes.

Briefly, then, economic security is no trade-off for economic risk taking. Both are required for healthy living, but settling for security and a job is a risky choice. It narrows all future choices and forecloses on certain avenues of being your own person as you get older.

BUILDING PERSONAL RELATIONSHIPS

What do you risk in relationships with other people? Two primary risk modes always seem to be present: "How much can I let this other person control and influence me?" "How close can I allow myself to get to other people?" [1] Whereas there are many subquestions, these are the most striking and the best indicators of a person's ability to take risks. Let's first consider the risk of allowing others to influence and control.

Holding On or Letting Go

As a middle manager you have supervisors who seek to influence you and you have bosses who seek to control you. Their inability to let go certainly influences you to practice what I call holding on. For example, how well can you delegate? One manager I know has what his employees call a penchant for detail. He's very benevolent and always has an open door for people's problems, but handles all sensitive (or even insensitive) matters that come to his attention. He cannot delegate because he will not risk what might happen as a result. Another manager doesn't let his wife know what his salary is. He gives her a number of dollars for household expenses but refuses to tell her his income. By doing this, he controls her and keeps her uncertain and in an unequal relationship.

Equal relationships in which one "lets go" are frightening to most managers, especially middle managers. They often feel unequal to executive management and, in order to maintain some status, they often attempt to maintain some omnipotence with their subordinates. The bad name that participative management has in many circles is not because of its failure but because of its partial success. Management is really afraid it might succeed and therefore decrease the need for management's omnipotence. Nothing is more interesting than to participate with management groups at several hierarchical levels in a single organization. Almost always, each level of management talks patronizingly of the subordinate group. Each group has to demonstrate its right to be boss of the next level. Such business cultures are seldom open to participative management where power, control, and influence are much more distributed, even though such equality would increase productivity.

In distributing power one must also distribute information. Many organizations filter fiscal information down the line. Production costs are protected from the eyes of the foreman charged with holding down costs. In some cases vice presidents are not allowed to sign off on fifty dollars. Little or no personal information is permitted to get abroad. Of course, there are limits to the spread of such information in public corporations where stockbrokers are often looking over the company shoulder. But mostly the secrecy syndrome is used to maintain the myth of executive management superiority and is supported at the next level by a conforming middle management.

This same middle management, in its need to impress the boss, may not only not share its power with others. It may even take that which its subordinates have away from them. The most glaringly bad management behavior of middle managers is when they substitute their name for their subordinate's on his work to enhance their image with top management. The number of middle managers who participate in this practice would astonish most organizations.

Most organizations don't reward executive or middle managers who share their authority. In fact, the trend is in the opposite direction, with centralized decision making becoming stronger. Thus less risk taking seems to be taking place. Until executive management includes middle managers in its loop, middle managers will feel that to include their subordinates has little reward for them. The result may be that middle managers will form unions to reduce the social and political power of management elitism.

Voluntarily giving away power and influence to others involves a degree of personal risk, and the manager must carefully assess the competence and trustworthiness of subordinates as well as ascertain how risky such a move will be in the eyes of top management. But the fact is that the sharing of power may lead to cooperation, while the hoarding of power often leads to competition and destructive conflict—an anathema to good teamwork and production.

Opaque Versus Transparent

The other major dimension of relating to people is how much we conceal rather than reveal who we are. Peculiarly enough, most managers think that the natural state of humanity, especially that of managers, is concealment rather than candor. Although concealment protects our vulnerabilities, it also prevents close relationships. The rewards from top management for candor and openness are vague enough to prevent most managers from taking much risk. The potential rewards of mental health and better functioning as a person seem just as vague when a manager faces an immediate choice of whether to let his weakness show to his colleagues.

Of course any manager needs to be aware of the situational factors when disclosing himself: the subject matter to be disclosed, his relation with the audience, the characteristics of the audience itself, and his own individual characteristics. Taking the

© 1970 Jules Feiffer, courtesy Publishers-Hall Syndicate

risk of becoming more transparent than opaque should be done situationally where possible, although managers have a generalized tendency to embrace either one or the other of those tendencies.

In marriage, some people are helped to be more candid with each other by open discussion of "sex" books. Such books have little intrinsic, artistic, or educational value, but they do provide vehicles which many people apparently need in order to come out of hiding from one another. Those who are transparent may not object to their spouses opening their mail, even mail marked personal. Consistent transparency with a spouse reduces the risk. No concealment means nothing to hide. It leads to a predictability in the relationship that provides an emotional security.

But how about transparency with colleagues at work? They don't have any wedding bands binding them to you till death do you part. Also, you probably don't want to invest as much of yourself in them as you do in your spouse. What can you do? You can, of course, take the old army routine and avoid getting involved with your colleagues. Some companies encourage that style. Others want to be one happy family, and stress picnics, Christmas parties, and so on. Others encourage a norm of immediate transparency between people within the normal constraints of the time on the job and the craziness of the particular people involved. But, whatever the choice, you are involved with other people and that means some measure of risk for you.

I remember one company president who finally decided that something had to be done about his vice president of manufacturing who was missing work, not supervising his employees, and, in general, causing plant gossip about his drinking. The president, who had a high regard for the vice president, called the vice president's wife and a counselor. He precipitated a confrontation during which the vice president saw himself as others saw him. He went to a treatment center and subsequently returned to the job. A retread, perhaps, but still very capable.

The president can take that risk, you say, but can you? The risk of getting involved with people at that level is great, but so are the rewards. It can leave you open to friendship and love in ways you might never have imagined. However, I caution you to move toward such risks with care. It involves skill, skill at disclosing yourself in ways not destructive to the other person. Rewarding relationships are never the result of chance, even though the original meeting might be. They involve the skill of knowing and being known, as well as the courage to be oneself among others.

The bureaucracies of today encourage self-protection and protection of the boss. This low risk posture really advocates a static risk of reducing loss without thought to gain. The middle manager who risks being transparent in relationships also takes the chance of being considered peculiar and needful. But work should provide a place where whole, rich, rewarding relationships can be found. Better to chance letting go too much and becoming too transparent. Holding on and opaqueness lead to the loss of the capacity to be a loving, mentally healthy and socialized person.

As noted earlier, if you do not seek deeper relationships with other people a certain atrophy takes place. People apart from people—for example, prisoners of war, self-styled recluses, or highly defensive individuals—lose the ability to relate significantly to others. They learn only to relate to themselves, becoming narcissistic and self-contained.

SELF-REALIZATION

Risk taking is necessary to realize personal potential. To a person who seeks self-realization, the risks seem small, while the fearful and faithless see these same risks as chasms to be leaped. The manager who takes breathtaking financial risks and is transparent in most relationships may no longer think of what she does as risk taking. Positive experiences with spouse, some friends, and sometimes employer all lead her to believe in her ability to judge the odds, risk no more than she can afford to lose, and avoid risking a lot for a little. Another person might be quite intimidated by the same set of circumstances that seems normal to this risk taker.

One of the most significant concerns of the self-realizer is being time competent. Time competent means having a good balance between being concerned for the future and aware of the past while living in the "now." When people don't take risks, they tend to prevent the development of those characteristics and thus do not realize their potential. One result of not risking, then, is to become time incompetent, afraid of the future and living in the subjunctive case.

Such time incompetents externalize their problems or do much wishful thinking. To externalize the cause of low risk taking, they say, "It's my wife (or husband)." "It's my job." Perhaps the most indefensible excuse people make is when they use their children: "I can't go back to school because of the children. They would have to drop music lessons, swimming lessons, be uprooted. . . ." Children have never been known to suffer deeply from materialistic privation. They have been known, however, to suffer from poor ego ideals with which to identify. They have also deeply resented having to be grateful for the gift of their parents' better years which they did not request be sacrificed for them.

I recall a story of a young man from the depression. His father had led a life of self-sacrifice for his family, having given up going to school and becoming a baker, even though at heart he was an artist and had wanted to go to Paris to study. Mother, feeling guilty herself, always reminded the son of how much his father had sacrificed. Then came the depression and the father lost his bakery. The son was on the verge of going to college and was quite willing to work his way through. He could not, however, bring himself to leave his parents and "selfishly" further himself. The result, years later, was a bitter mailman. The model his father established would be passed to each generation. The message is unmistakable. Each generation lives for the next, rather than for itself. As the book of Jeremiah suggests, "the fathers have eaten sour grapes and the children's teeth are set on edge."

Why am I relating this story? Because such sacrifice for children is, for most people, only an inept excuse. It is face-saving behavior for the fearful who can't take risks. They use their children as scapegoats for their failures. Their children, if wise, will understand. If not, they will carry the burden of having held back their father, who is really holding back himself.

It is like the story of the 40-year-old quality control manager in a factory who told his doctor that he had always wanted to be a physician. His doctor, realizing his patient was bored with life and steadily becoming personally and physically obsolete, said, "Why don't you go now? You've got enough salted away, and with Martha working, you could do it." The manager replied, "But, Doctor, I'd be 50 years old by the time I finished my training." The doctor replied, "How old will you be if you don't go through training?" In other words, all of us, but especially middle managers, live in the subjunctive case. Our speech is peppered with, I would, but, I should . . . , I might . . . , if, if, if—a way of saving face when backing down. Growth comes from engaging the here and now, taking the risk.

In this chapter I presented one excellent reason for flexing your risk muscles: your ability to risk can atrophy just as your ability to walk. The more you try, the greater your capacity to succeed.

There are two big areas in a person's life where the risk of not risking looms large. One is the field of making money. Money must work for you, not the other way around. That means taking a risk. Why take a chance? Because making money is stimulating. It keeps your energies creative and focuses you on producing something of merit, rather than on just marking time until retirement. Besides, money is fun to have and fun to make. Money broadens the avenues and smooths the paths.

The other important area is that of risk in personal relationships. Two primary modes of risk are involved here: holding on versus letting go and opaqueness versus transparency. The first of these raises the issue of control. Letting go in a relationship is frightening for a middle manager. Loss of control in any amount leaves him threatened by subordinates and by the fear that his boss will no longer be sufficiently impressed. The risk of giving away power is great and must be carefully done. When it pays off, that risk can change destructive competition and conflict to cooperation and "working the problem."

The second mode is essentially that of self-revelation. Can the middle manager risk being seen as vulnerable? Such a decision to be open should be cautiously done, at least at first, and done on a situation-by-situation basis. It takes skill to risk successfully in personal relationships. Why risk if it's such a tricky thing? Dare to be open because this is the only way to find the rewarding relationships you need to become a whole person. Share your humanity with others to enrich your own life and theirs. The greater the risk, the greater the possible payoffs.

7 | Risk Taking and Religious Faith

RELIGION doesn't fare too well in today's press, whether it be conventional, such as the National Council of Churches of Christ, or otherwise (Jesus freaks). However, there are still a good many friends of conventional and unconventional religious movements. Many people—humanists, humanistic psychologists, and just people on the street—still espouse some strong personal convictions. If religion is a disease of overdependence on a projected omnipotent power that doesn't really exist, as some writers (namely, Freud) have said, it seems to be incurable. I'm certainly glad, because religion in its deepest sense resolves one's needs to be dependent, which, in turn, allows greater freedom to take risks. Those without some commitment to nonrelative human and ethical values, or to a personal God that is omnipresent, will soon find themselves awash in a sea of relative probabilities which will undermine creative risk taking, replacing faith with fear.

But, perhaps you are saying, "What's a chapter on religion doing in a management book?" Very simple. The man or woman on the job is the same one who is at home, in church, at the beach, in the workshop, at the local bistro, or at the country club. He or she is a whole person. Love, joy, meaning, collecting Christmas plates, camping, and all the other activities that make up being a human being aren't left at the company gate on Monday morning.

This chapter deals with the themes of the courage to be, the courage to become, and the courage to die. All are religious themes. All are underlying concerns, which, when dealt with, lead to creative living and risk taking for middle managers in their corporations.

Before going on to the meat of this chapter I must state a disclaimer, a caveat for the reader who still considers work, success, and purity as equal virtues. Such a philosophy dominated the birth of the industrial revolution. William H. Whyte, Jr., in his classic *The Organization Man*, says:

If we pick up popular fiction around the 1870s we find the Protestant Ethic in full flower. It was plain that the hero's victories over his competition and his accumulation of money were synonymous with godliness. The hero was shown in struggle with the environment, and though good fortune was an indispensable assist, it was less an accident than a reward directed his way by just providence. This didn't always go without saying, but it could. As late as the turn of the century the ethic remained so unquestioned that the moralizing could be left out entirely. Heroes were openly, exultantly materialistic and, if they married the boss's daughter or pushed anyone around on the way up, this was as it should be.[1]

In 1959 I visited a Plymouth factory in Detroit. I was part of a group being orientated to the problems and dynamics of building cars and managing companies. Because the group were clergymen, management apparently wanted to convince us of how seriously it took religion, although it never actually said so. As it happened, we enjoyed listening to a line foreman and a middle manager, and were promised an interview with a member of top management. We also talked with people on the line. Our hosts were gracious and it was a growth experience.

However, in the middle of all this, a man was ushered into the seminar room who was billed as the Billy Graham of the auto industry. For an hour and a half we listened to the virtues of hard work and obedience, combined with high sales volume, good profit picture, clean lives, and the guidance of God. After one particularly descriptive passage on his trip to the Southwest and his talks to YMCAs and Rotary clubs, I asked him why he kept saying, "We then went . . . ," or "We said to them . . . ," or "We took the car. . . ." I naïvely asked if he had taken his wife with him. He replied that the "we" meant he and Jesus, because Jesus was with him wherever he went—in the showroom, on the used car lot, in the YMCA. Apparently his postscripts on letters also reflected this business partnership he and Jesus and, by extension, Plymouth had developed.

I'm still thunderstruck by the response, and reject out of hand God's forwarding the fortune of this or any other private or publicly held corporation, government, nation, or institution developed by human beings. Engine Charlie's 1950 phrase, "What's good for General Motors is good for the country," is far less presumptuous than the auto manufacturer's use of Elmer Gantryism to move cars. This chapter isn't about that kind of religion.

THE COURAGE TO BE

Sometimes it doesn't pay to get up in the morning, any morning, and some people don't. They are sick, old, afraid, bored—suffering some kind of condition that takes the courage to be. A dear friend of mine, a moneyman and once a fine banker, lost the function of both kidneys seven years ago. Since then, he has been kept alive through dialysis. He and his family have had little sleep, much pain, a falling away of fair-weather friends, and a disintegrating financial situation. In the midst of this, against all odds, he is still alive physically, mentally, and spiritually. Though scared and bewildered by the visitation of such tragedy, this modern Job still has faith in himself and the source of his existence. For him, as well as for me, that source is a personal God. Others have various names for what gives them the exceptional confidence that seems to fly in the face of such adversity, for what allows one to take what others consider too great a risk.

As you can guess, I'm fairly conventional in my ideas about what strengthens a person. Let me share with you some convictions about how strength is maintained.

First of all, courage to be means you can afford to be generous. Some years ago a businessman gave up a partnership, and, in the course of the disassociation, he gave the significant accounts to his ex-partner. He made this gesture because he felt the partner would have a more difficult time finding new accounts. As I talked with him, it became obvious that he did not think of this as a personal sacrifice. Rather, he knew he could produce new accounts, get new customers. He could afford to be generous. Such generosity strengthened his self-confidence.

Courage to be is also maintained by "keeping it all together." In this context keeping it together means keeping your value system congruent, not compartmentalizing your life. A manager I once knew interviewed a prospective employee. In the course of the interview he found out that the man had a wife and family but also had a hidden mistress and children. He suggested that the man seek elsewhere for employment. He told him, "I don't pay you enough money to support two families. You'll soon have to steal from me. Then, too, if you'll cheat on your wife, you'll cheat on me."

It may be that he was wrong. The man may indeed not have let his left hand know what the right hand was doing. However, in either case, his lack of a consolidated life reflected adversely on his capacity to be straight with colleagues, clients, and friends. There is, in fact, a self-righteousness that comes from consolidation that is obnoxious on occasion, but which provides the obnoxious ones with inordinate strength that makes their fellows jealous. A superness accompanies people with the courage to be that often puts off those who are near them or who are fearful.

The greatest advantage of being a consolidated person is that your energy is not wasted keeping parts of your life separated from each other. A Watergate scandal, a Profumo affair, and other myriad complex scandals are energy sapping. A person cannot focus his or her energies externally when so much has to be used up internally. This ability to use personal horsepower is important because intelligence alone isn't enough for risk taking. Men and women such as Jesus, Gandhi, Florence Nightingale, and Joan of Arc are not remembered for their intelligence but for their singleness of purpose, their consolidated lives. Thus, a high risk taker may simply be a consolidated person of great energy and singleness of purpose.

Also, I honestly believe that a person of religious strengths with the courage to be never prays "up"; supplication isn't the game. Cries of happiness, despair, loneliness, fear, and so forth are quite normal, but the courage to be means the courage to be alone, in your own skin, in a universe that is a mixture of loving and hateful forces. The Christian faith presents a God who can do little, who is pinioned to a cross by the powers of the world. The message I get is, "You can handle the same thing, so don't expect any quick and dirty miracles. God is with you in the sense he's been there too, but you are on your own in this life."

I believe that. I don't look up anymore. I look inside myself for the strength that has already been given to me. I support the continual development of our stewardship of the world through the evolvement of greater human skill and technological resources. I look to my loved ones for support, confrontation, and a reason to be. I look at my work as an opportunity to offer my energies alongside others in the human enterprise. I look for the kind of success that can be defined as ". . . the progressive realization of a worthy ideal," perhaps many ideals. I do not look up, for, as Bishop Robinson said in *Honest to God*, "The sky is empty." [2] We are alone in the sense that there is no great benevolent sugar daddy to spring us from our human frailties or to perform other "acts of God" as defined by insurance companies. To face up to that and to be strong is to have the courage to be.

THE COURAGE TO BECOME

Once you are up in the morning you can steer a survival course close to the shore, always keeping land in sight. You may also venture further, depending on the stars, a compass, or a damn good sense of direction. People with the courage to become have this sense of direction and use it.

Their sense of direction is not usually a highly intellectual process. Rather, they follow opportunities. Given choices, they choose, and rarely do they make the choice with the lowest potential payoff. One middle manager was trained as a lawyer. His job called for little direct application of his training. I asked him when he decided to stop being a lawyer to do what he was doing. He replied that he had never left law. He had simply followed what he wanted and the result was his present position. He had added to something, not given up anything.

Over the past few years disenchanted clergy have asked me for advice about leaving the ministry. I've always said first off, "What is it you want to do that will give you a full life?" Without exception they have replied, "I don't know. Just anything. I can't stand what I'm doing." My advice is always, "That is not enough of a reason to quit doing it. You should not *leave* anything. You should always be *going to* something." I don't believe I'm quibbling with words here but, rather, suggesting the spiritual posture of the person with the courage to become. This person is always in the process of being created, re-created, and renewed.

Excellent

Having a sense of direction doesn't mean you always know where you are or that you always will choose the right path. You may well drop a perfectly good job in production to try your hand in the new long-range planning department with a newly hired ambitious vice president who soon gets into enough hot water to lose his job and wipe yours out too. You may decide to leave the Connecticut plant of your company and move to Florida as requested, only to lose your seniority while others move up the ladder in Connecticut.

But in both cases the reverse may also have happened. The new vice president might turn the sales trend straight up with accurate forecasting and blind luck. As the new president next year, he'll want you around. Or the Florida plant may get the biggest contract ever given by the Department of Defense to the aerospace industry, resulting in increased responsibility for you. Consider the odds. The courage to become means taking creative risks, following your sense of direction.

There is a touching story of Jesus asking a man to join his disciples. The man was a responsible citizen and a good son. To paraphrase, he replied, "I'd love to do it but first let me bury my father." Jesus was disappointed and went on without him. Why? Because the man looked back. He was not in touch with his opportunity as a man with direction is. He was not a bad man but he was not prepared to become, to have a singleness of purpose.

Part of this sense of direction comes from operating out of a sense of organic time, or time in the sense of kairos rather than chronos. Chronos is cyclical time where a specific time segment is made up of equal and uniform, smaller segments of time. It is time that is created by people but has no connection with growth, feelings, history. In chronos there is no sense of the right time, the fullness of time, or a bad time. Those terms refer to kairos time. To oversimplify, kairos time is sensing when circumstances are such that the odds are propitious. One man I know turned down three jobs in a company over the period of four years. At the end of the fourth year they offered him the presidency. He took it. Studebaker put out its postwar cars at the wrong time. In 1974 they would have been sensational.

A sense of timing is critical to the courage to become. If you lack this sense, the odds are much against you on high risk opportunities. Of course, all of us have or have had that sense at one point. It is equipment that comes in every new human model, but if unused, neglected, or denied, it atrophies. Once out of touch with the spirit that gives a sense of direction, you will find it hard to regain. In religious parlance it is akin to losing your soul. You give up your birthright for security, as did Esau for a mess of porridge. Such is the case with many middle managers, the forgotten people of management.

Most middle managers need to reactivate their faith in themselves — the courage to be — and to reassess their sense of direction and timing in their lives — the courage to become. "For what will it profit a man, if he gains the whole world and forfeits his life?"

THE COURAGE TO DIE

I don't have much of an imagination, therefore, I don't really view the promise of life after death with much certainty. As the Christian creed says, there is some *hope* of a resurrection, but as to certainty, I guess I'm of too practical a mind. I can't seem to follow Paul's tortuous arguments regarding spiritual and physical bodies after death. Even more confusing are the esoteric states and complicated postdeath theories of reincarnation and of Eastern religions in general. In the light of so little certainty, perhaps the best suggestion is "to live in this life so that you will be worthy of the life to come."

Personally, I interpret that statement to mean you should live fully now, because if there is a life after death and you have not lived fully now, you won't know how to use the next life either. So many people are always looking for happiness "later on." When I get out of school, maybe . . . when I get married, maybe . . . when the kids leave home, maybe . . . when I retire, maybe . . . when I die, maybe. . . . Life is to be lived fully now. To have the courage to die means living fully now without fear. In Christian theology that approach is called realized eschatology, or having the last things now, not in the by and by. To have the courage to die is to overcome the fear of bodily harm and the fear of separation from people. Living fully is living with those fears at manageable levels.

I am not suggesting that one should be foolish in risking bodily harm. Smoking, excessive eating and drinking, and using various narcotics and hallucinogens are all to be avoided on real pain of death. What I'm talking about is the psychological fear that keeps you from exposing your body to punishment when necessary. We can all remember some incident not unlike that which happened in Kew Gardens, New York, in 1962. A woman was raped and beaten within earshot of at least 50 people who made no effort to help her. They were afraid for their lives and for their bodies. The people who closed their hearts gave up something of their consolidation. They lost some of their sense of direction, their humanity. They let the fact that they were afraid to die intimidate them.

Once the world can frighten and intimidate you, using bodily harm as blackmail, you've given up your autonomy and a source of your risk taking. Risk taking comes from not being [very] afraid to live and not being [very] afraid to die. I bracketed "very" because appropriate fear of particular circumstances is quite normal and part of determining the odds on any risk. But excessive fear of losing your life or health can impair adequate living and creative risk taking. The New Testament never suggests that death is not omnipresent. It does suggest that for those of faith the sting of death is removed.

What difference does it actually make that the sting of death is removed? It means to no longer carry an overriding fear of loss and extinction. Perhaps the best illustration of the benefits can be seen in many older people whose friends have long gone on and who obviously not only don't fear death but long for it. I recall one elderly woman who asked the parson to pray for her death. He was reluctant but did say a prayer, compromising slightly by saying, ". . . and if it be thy will, Oh Father, take thy servant to Thee." At this juncture the woman broke in, saying, "Now!"

Being beyond the clutches of fear often lets older people speak their minds. Sometimes because of this talent they seem addled to those who still fear the sting of death. Perhaps we've developed a society where middle managers and others can be pushed out of the workforce before they can express their newly found autonomy within corporate life. A man or woman who doesn't fear death also doesn't fear the president, being fired, or being hurt. He or she can no longer be bribed by pension plans nor made afraid by dire warnings.

The sting of death is also failure. Failure is part of the risk taker's daily bread. Perhaps over the years the risk takers will receive more loaves than crumbs. The story of most successful business people, however, is one of several or even many failures. Failure is a form of death. It is an arrow into the courage to be and to become. It threatens to annihilate the risk taker. Therefore, as we pointed out in Chapter 3, people fearing failure will be far more likely to avoid risk.

Failure is felt physically. The stomach becomes acidic, gas forms in the bowels, butterflies appear in the gut and seem uncontrollable. Sleep becomes fitful. At times, depression consumes the psyche. Hyperactivity in meaningless tasks may also occur. All are signs of the body's response to fear of extinction. If you would avoid unpleasantness of this sort at any cost, the sting of death may well inhibit possible risks you might take for yourself, your family, or your company. That kind of problem can't be easily surveyed, and certainly is no fault of top management. It's yours. Just as the courage to be and to become are the individual's decision, so is the courage to die. You have to do it alone.

The other significant barrier to having the courage to die relates to people in your life. The psychiatrists call it separation anxiety. We all have it, from the baby who cries when its mother leaves the house to friends who cry at my funeral. While these are more dramatic instances, middle managers face little separation anxieties each day. They are a fear of death which implies permanent separation from others. Let's examine a few potential trouble spots.

Managers with great fear of moving, either from their present position or from home, tend to have great separation anxiety. In fact, some managers when told they must relocate will make everyone angry at them so that leaving will be easier. "Old Joe was a great guy until they promoted him to New York. Then he got uppity with all of us. You wouldn't believe the outrageous ways he treated everyone."

Going-away parties are like funerals. They are meant to allay the separation anxiety we all feel at losing significant relationships. Perhaps when people get divorced there should be a party for friends of the divorcer and divorcee to work through the feeling of loss — a kind of death — we all feel in the loss of loved ones.

Middle managers who decide to take risks within their personal lives and within their company are immediately going to face a loss of friends and temporary periods of top management disapproval. And potentially they may have to separate themselves from the most intense of those relationships. Sometimes this is a friend; sometimes it is a company. The concept I am using here is one coined by Eric Erikson. He calls it distantiation. It is the ability to separate yourself from people who need you so much that they are potentially destructive. It is the ability to resist giving up your autonomy for the promise of another person's regard. It is the ability to withdraw from a company which consistently demeans you, from groups that insult you, or from people who use closeness to undermine your courage to be and become.

One couple I know has what would be regarded as conventional marriage by those people who cohabit rather than marry, supposedly "keeping their freedom." However, this couple is married because they want to be, and each is capable of distantiation were it to the advantage of either. They are able to invest without fear of losing or destroying each other. They have the courage to become, because they do not fear separation.

The low risk tendencies of middle managers today may not be that they are committed and obedient creatures. Rather, the problem may be that they lack the courage to die, lack the courage to become, or lack the courage to be. Unable to risk, they may bind themselves to jobs and friends that will steadily erode their faith in themselves by the time they are 40. One can only invest life, energy, love, and all one's power in relationships to the degree that one feels free to create distance in those relationships, to the degree that one can retain personal integrity above all.

This chapter dealt with religion, and with the whole person each of us is when we arrive on the scene at work each day. Religion, in the final analysis, frees us from our fears to take risks we might otherwise avoid. My religion is based on a belief in a personal God. Whatever the basis for yours, it will provide you with a foundation for risking if it encompasses these three factors: the courage to be, the courage to become, and the courage to die.

The courage to be is that feeling of exceptional confidence in the midst of trials and tribulations that makes us act instead of merely react to our troubles. It helps us stick our necks out for ourselves, gives us the freedom to be generous at our own expense, and keeps our lives consolidated. A person with the courage to be believes in personal power and authority, and never prays for magical solutions.

The courage to become lets us follow opportunities and see choices as an additive process, rather than the constant necessity to give something up. If we have the courage to become, then we have direction and a continual impetus to grow and to be continually re-created. The key to the courage to become is intuitive timing — kairos, rather than chronos.

The courage to die is necessary for living life to the fullest. If we can overcome unreasonable fears of bodily harm, fears of separation from people, and fears of failure, then there is very little we cannot do. Even in the business world, we must be able to risk physical pain. We must certainly be able to distantiate from even our loved ones if it means preserving our integrity. We must surely accept failure as the training ground for the successful risk taker.

Having all three factors gives us the kind of special qualities we probably admire right now in the next person. Singleness of purpose (courage to be), direction for action (courage to become), and a certain kind of unflinching attitude (courage to die) are the keys to the kinds of personal risk taking we are talking about. They spell success.

8 | Are All Middle Managers Uncreative?

MANY MIDDLE MANAGERS will answer the question, "Are you creative?" negatively. Some may be right about themselves. Most are wrong. Middle managers are no different along this dimension than most people. The problem is that they are most often in situations that demand repetition rather than creativity, conformity rather than diversity. If their actions are unconventional top management sees them as unpredictable. If they try to experiment with job redesign, their employees are suspicious and wonder what's in it for them.

These restrictions on experimenting with new ideas are imposed on most everyone from early childhood on. Do you remember how difficult it was to keep inside the black lines when you were watercoloring in the first grade? Daydreaming was a sin. Telling fanciful stories was lying. To pretend was O.K., until a certain age when it became embarrassing. Sexual fantasies were no-no's, and getting out of line—the line to the cafeteria, the line to the washroom, the line to come in from the playground, *any line*—was considered bad behavior.

Middle management's job of carnival juggler is not conducive to getting out of line. The middle manager is the nexus of various forces that want coordination, implementation, and follow-through, pretty much in the same old ways. Is that statement true, or is it simply an unverified assumption middle managers have made? Is it possible that top management and first-line supervisors want to be pushed more? The evidence is unclear as to how much creativity top management wants. But what is clear is that creativity always involves the company in risk taking. Top management usually has very clear policies regarding the attendant risks that creativity causes. Every company says it wants creativity. Few want the associated risks—which, by the way, is sensible. Why risk if you can have the same thing without risk? But, of course, you can't.

In this chapter I want to show how creativity and the tendency to risk are associated. I'd then like to develop some organization styles using these two factors to determine what certain middle managers are like.

DEFINING CREATIVITY AND RISK TAKING

I am defining creativity as the ability to think up unconventional ideas. Those ideas may be as mundane as turning eggshells into little faces or as sublime as Athelstan Spilhaus' floating cities in the Atlantic Ocean. They may be as practical as the saltshaker or as far out as an astronomic equation. But in all cases the common denominator is the unconventionality of the idea. It challenges contemporary practices or thought.

Risk taking here means the willingness to tenaciously push your ideas on top management and your colleagues at some (how much?) personal risk to yourself. There is always resistance to change, and creativeness always involves change. My wife asked me why soda pop had not been sold in cans before it was; beer was sold in cans much earlier. I responded that the costs of changing the production and marketing methods may have been prohibitive. Regardless of whether I am right about the specific situation, the point is still valid—creativity means change, and change involves increased expense and risk taking. Who knows if people will drink pop from cans?

RISK STYLES AND THEIR EFFECTS

Everyone, no matter how he responds in day-to-day situations, still develops an unmistakable risk style over the years. That style may be high, moderate, or low risk taking. Once you determine what that style is, the odds are 20 to 1 that you can predict your own and management's response to a proposal. This is valuable knowledge to have.

To put it another way, my hypothesis is that there is a normal curve of risk takers (see Figure 2). They range from those who are completely other-directed, taking all their cues from the desires of the organization (16 percent), to those who are almost totally inner-directed, taking their cues from no one but themselves (16 percent). (Researchers kept in company basements make up this latter group.) The other 68 percent of us fall between these extremes, taking, more or less, our cues from our environment and from our own convictions, needs, and interests.

Your style may vary, depending to some degree on the particular corporation in which you work. However, if your behavior were plotted on a scattergram, you would show a central risk-taking tendency. For example, in Figure 3 each dot represents a decision made over a two-year period by Mr. X and Mr. Y. The riskiness of each manager's decisions was the consensus of his employees. According to the judgment of his team, Manager X exhibits low to moderately risky decision making; Manager Y's employees rate him as moderate to high. Each has an individual style. Thus, depending on the output, whether a product or service, whether professional or commercial, or whatever part of the organization, each can also be plotted on its risk-taking propensity.

Creativity is measured by originality, by an ability to break away from conventional ideas. In fact, originality is about the

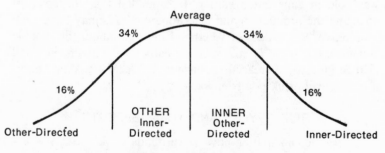

Figure 2.   Risk curve.

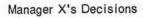

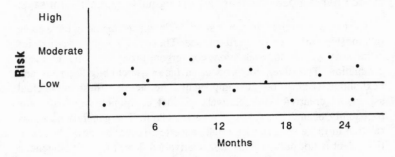

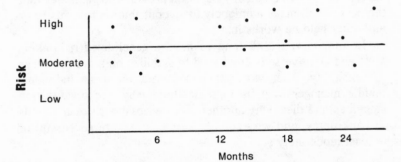

Figure 3.   Scattergrams of two risk-taking styles.

only criterion for creativity that researchers can agree on. A few of us live in a phantasmogoric world of wildly imaginative ideas, and some of us are at the opposite extreme, entirely out of touch with the preconscious, or daydream life. Using an attitude scale I developed to measure people's creative propensities, I have come to the conclusion that most of us lie between these extremes.

"Genius" seems to be the only word available to describe the really creative thinker. It's the word we use to distinguish an Einstein from a bright quiz-show participant. It's unfortunate that we don't have another word, because "genius" implies that creativity is related to intelligence. Yet there is little evidence that this is so. We have all known employees who had highly original ideas but only average intelligence. Many of the so-called brightest people never had an original thought. Taylor says:

> Certain intellectual characteristics, for instance, appear to have some relationship with creative performance. These fall within the categories of memory, cognition, evaluation, convergent production and divergent production. The divergent production factors, including fluencies and flexibilities, seem to be most important. The fact that these intellectual aspects of creativity are relatively distinct components indicates the probability of multiple types of creative talent. The generally low correlation of these factors with intelligence test scores suggests that creative talent is not only various, but relatively different from intelligence.[1]

IQ may be a predictor of academic success, and a safe bet for success on certain kinds of jobs, but it provides no guarantee that the person will make a uniquely fresh contribution to industry or any other field he works in.

In summary, we all tend to have a generalized risk-taking style and creative sense that tend to stabilize on a normal curve of sensitivity. The two factors measured within an individual middle manager help us to understand why one organization stagnates and dies, why another takes excessive risks and lands in bankruptcy, and why countless other firms are successful or at least moderately so.

A TYPOLOGY OF CREATIVE RISK TAKERS

Figure 4 is the matrix on which we can plot the various types of middle manager risk-taking styles. The perpendicular scale designates the degree to which one is generally a high or low risk taker. The horizontal scale is, from left to right, the creative abilities. There are eight types. The four in the corners are people less influenced by their fellows. They are toward the 16 percent of the population on both factors—high or low (remember the percentages under the normal curve). When socialized, they tend to behave in the more other-directed version of their styles. Thus the repeater may become a modifier; the challenger, a practicalizer; the innovator, a synthesizer; and the dreamer, a planner.[2]

We will discuss each type of risk taker in turn, giving the general characteristics as well as the contributions and weaknesses. For a summary of all eight, see Table 1.

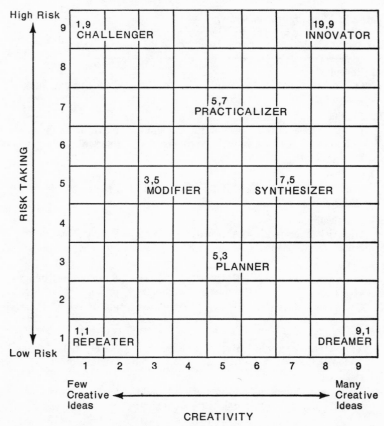

Figure 4. The Creatrix.

1,1 The Repeater

Repeaters are other-directed persons who have few imaginative ideas and seldom entertain unconventional approaches. They tend to reject what they have not thought of, and usually think what they have thought of before. Repeaters seldom see the need for planning because the past generally holds the best lessons. They usually support control methods, standardization, time studies, industrial engineering methods, quality control, and simplicity of product line. They resist new systems and techniques such as computerization and cybernetics.

Table 1. *The eight risk styles.*

RISK STYLE	CONTRIBUTION	WEAKNESS
1,1 Repeater Other-directed, uncreative	Good for routine tasks	Tends to get stuck
3,5 Modifier In the middle of the risk curve, somewhat creative	Good for constant, little improvements	Never finds the brilliant solution
1,9 Challenger Consistent risk taker with few new ideas	Willing to agitate for change	May be too destructive
5,7 Practicalizer High risk taker, moderately creative	Action oriented, gets things done	Rarely plays the long shot
9,9 Innovator High risk taker, very creative	Responsible for all major nonincremental success in industry	Radical, may be impatient with corporate reality
7,5 Synthesizer Very creative, moderate risk taker	Highly creative, but controllable	Rarely risks for the breakthrough
9,1 Dreamer High creativity, very low risk taker	Little direct benefit unless taken in hand by a high risk taker	Underachiever
5,3 Planner Other-directed, moderately creative	Can make creative ideas operable	Can't implement ideas

Contributions. The repeater may not be offended by repetitive tasks—filing, accounting, stocking shelves—that no one else wants to do. He doesn't care, all other benefits of the job being equal to others within the organization. The repeater is often the backbone of the organization, providing the control and predictive functions necessary to good management.

Weaknesses. Repeaters get stuck in ruts. They continually perform tasks that no longer need doing. They are the janitors who sweep a floor that is now cleaned by air filtration. They are the company presidents who can't really treat the newly acquired subsidiary as a member of the corporate family because the subsidiary's product is in a different industry. I suppose a final weakness is that repeaters are seldom valued by the organization, despite the fact that without them the organization would certainly falter, systems couldn't stay institutionalized, and quality of production might fall.

3,5 The Modifier

The modifier is somewhat creative and pretty well in the center of the normal curve of risk taking. The modifier takes what is and adds to it. The modifier rarely discovers a new use for an old item, but he might move two factory machines closer together so that one person could run both at the same time. A modifier paints furniture a color that shows less dirt; he adds paragraphs to manuscripts.

Contributions. Such a person can usually be counted on for the constant little improvements so necessary for lowering production, marketing, or management costs. He will suggest turning a form upside down for greater ease of use. He will suggest using different molds for casting or different material for filling teeth. While rarely exceptionally creative, the modifier will take moderate risks and install what he wants – and then tell someone. However, he is quite willing to return to the old way if top management so desires. He always provides fairly safe, incremental improvements.

Weaknesses. Perhaps the greatest weakness of the modifier is that he can never be counted on for the brilliant solution. He also can't be counted on to fight very hard for his own suggestions. Because of an apparent need to be liked or to go along, and because the proposed alterations are rarely threatening to others, modifiers are usually valued by any organization they are in.

1,9 The Challenger

Challengers are consistent risk takers with few new ideas. They are always discontent with the slowness of change. In one sense they are nihilists. Challengers are the people in the group who almost always have an excellent analysis of why something won't work. People are always telling them, "Don't criticize this idea unless you have a better one." Well, they may not have any wine in their glasses, but they know what people will drink. They rarely have an idea, and most of what they hear fails to appeal to them. They seem almost to want change for change's sake. Their energy always lies in wait to be used by those who have creative ideas but little stomach for risk taking. They are like the repeater in that they lack new ideas, but are self-directed and motivated like the innovator.

Contributions. Challengers serve the organization in various ways. First, they expose sacred cows. In other words, over the years, management creates an organizational climate where an employee knows certain processes and practices are not discussed. It may be that top management has the best parking places and that seniority counts for nothing. A middle manager of ten years of service may get bumped from the garage for a new vice president. Certain key clients may be assigned to the boss's inexperienced son or daughter, who becomes an instant success. The challenger will ask openly, "What the hell's going on?"

Weaknesses. While the challenger calls a spade a spade, he may also destroy where destruction wasn't needed. A nearly retired muddling middle manager may be forced to quit six months from retirement because a challenger may agitate to send him to the showers. Tolerated a little longer, the muddling middle manager would have left with self-esteem and retirement intact, as well as leaving other employees with a sense of mattering. A program that needs time to prove itself may not get the chance if the challenger is allowed his way. The challenger, as you can imagine, is not the most popular member of the organization.

5,7 The Practicalizer

Practicalizers are high on risk taking and moderately creative. They are as creative as the planner, but because they will take more risks in the organization, they make ideas work. A socialized challenger tends to practicalize new approaches. Practicalizers are often effective managers. They like taking ideas and driving them through the bureaucratic walls of the organization. Because they are moderately creative, they can recognize the gifts of the innovator, who tends to be socially unacceptable, and of the synthesizer, the dreamer, and the planner, who are preoccupied with the product rather than its implementation. They know that someone, namely, themselves, will be able to convince top management of the need to make major changes.

Contributions. The practicalizer is action-oriented and gets things done. Often the practicalizer is the only middle manager who can get a change accepted. They will take the risks, up to a point, because they are confident of the possibilities. They are, however, also the organization's politicians. President Johnson once said, "Politics is the art of the possible." The practicalizer rarely gets confused between what is the right thing to do creatively and what is implementable. They will always compromise for the "possible."

Weaknesses. Perhaps the only weakness of true practicalizers is that they will sell out the supercreative people in the crunch and thus sometimes miss the big payoffs. Practicalizers rarely play the long shot. They are the George Allen's of the business world. Today is the day to win. They will trade their first draft choices of tomorrow for a winner today. But by so doing, they may risk losing the superstar a draft choice would have brought.

9,9 The Innovator

The innovator is very high on both risk taking and creativity. She always has a new idea and is willing to give up her job if she can't get the organization's support. To others, she seems to be just like the challenger—outspoken, hard to influence, and of a single mind. Unlike the challengers, however, innovators always have a better mousetrap. Innovators are full of alternatives, and any one of them may be better than anything the organization is currently doing, but startup costs are prohibitive. But they rarely accept that as an excuse.

Innovators usually sense a breakthrough product, which must be accepted from time to time if an organization is to compete. Breakthroughs initially are never popular to an organization because they involve new technology and all kinds of changes.

Innovators know this and will still fight fiercely for the break-through's acceptance. Innovators have to hang tough to find acceptance for their ideas. They continue to believe when no one else does.

Contributions. All major, nonincremental successes in American industry are the result of innovators. Henry Ford is perhaps the most commonly used example of a man with an idea. But if it were not for Galileo, we'd still have a flat world. If Freud hadn't fought the Vienna medical profession, we might never have discovered the unconscious. Elizabeth Stanton, Lucretia Mott, Martha Wright, and Mary Ann McClintock fought for suffrage for American women—a significant innovation. Today, when innovators can't find acceptance of their ideas within a corporation, they find capital and start their own. They will risk. They will risk more than they can afford to lose, from the point of view of most people.

Weaknesses. The innovator may become so fixed on one idea that she cannot accept "wait a while." The sense of correctness an innovator feels about certain potential breakthroughs is so strong that she can't and doesn't want to see implementation problems. When what she wants is not forthcoming, the innovator may well develop the paranoid idea that the organization is against her and that plots are made in executive suites to block her. While always admired and probably feared, the innovator is a radical and therefore is rarely at the head of the most-liked list.

7.5 The Synthesizer

The synthesizer is quite creative and generally moderate in risk taking. They are idea people. They practicalize conceptually what others think. They take unlikely combinations of people, programs, or products and devise a new entity. Their talents are taking other people's ideas, adding some of their own, and making them fit existing situations. Their ideas will never be as practical or as easily implemented as those of the practicalizer, but they will develop high-quality ideas that are just short of a break-through. Like the modifier, synthesizers only like moderate risks. They would rather trust that the ideas will carry their own weight to induce change. This position makes them appear to be dreamers or planners to those who mistake how far they will go to sell their ideas.

Data 100 Corporation and International Timesharing Corporation are examples of synthesizing organizations. Companies such as IBM Corporation and Xerox Corporation are noted for being innovators, just as the auto industry is for being modifiers.

Contributions. A synthesizer is often the most highly valued of creative people. They are company gods first and creators second. In other words, their moderate risk taking makes them controllable, unlike the innovator. They are planners and organizers, and often function as peacemakers between warring factions. They see combinations of functions, processes, and people that others don't see. New organization charts or production flows challenge their ingenuity.

Good marketing managers dealing with tailor-made products or seminars tend to be synthesizers. They are always combining the needs of the customer with the talents (and potential talents, if they have to hire them) and resources of the company. They are also usually liked, although not always understood. They are socialized innovators.

Weaknesses. The only major blind spot of the synthesizers is an inability to risk all for a breakthrough. They believe in incremental breakthroughs. They are no SST lovers. They want the better jet for their customers now, not later. This so-called weakness is, of course, no weakness in the organization that has an innovator. If there is no innovator, then the synthesizer's new ideas, always appealing and usually marketable, will prevail.

9,1 The Dreamer

The most underutilized middle manager is the dreamer. She is in the upper 16 percent in creativity and the lower 16 percent of risk takers. Her head is full of unusual ideas that, because of her lack of aggressiveness, look like crackpot schemes. The dreamer often has repeater-like jobs, jobs that take little risk and offer her time to think.

At home the dreamer may be an inventor, a tinkerer, or a TV night owl. She always has a better idea, but rarely suggests it unless asked. The dreamer is basically discontent with the company she knows could grow. She is, however, afraid to let loose and convince the company that her approach is better for all.

Contributions. From an organization's point of view there is little direct benefit from having a dreamer in the organization, unless a practicalizer is her boss. Even then, getting the talents of the dreamer to be anything more than unmined gold may be more than an organization can tolerate. The dreamer may adequately fill a repeater niche, but this gross underuse of talent takes its toll on the person and the product.

Weaknesses. The major weakness is obvious. The dreamer is an underachiever. Being so other-directed and conforming, she may set regressive organization patterns that make the risk taking of the challenger, the practicalizer, and the innovator even riskier. The other extreme, a company full of bright, creative dreamers, is headed toward business disaster.

5,3 The Planner

The planner tends to be other-directed. Not as creative as the dreamer or synthesizer, the planner nevertheless thinks of ways in which creative ideas might be utilized. Like the practicalizer, the planner wants creative ideas to be operable but he doesn't have the risk-taking capacity. The result is that planners can make the plans but not force them through. They often find themselves in a planning department, in an architectural firm, teaching in a university, or making feasibility studies in a consulting firm.

Contributions. The planner can and does develop alternatives for the corporation. If asked to force a change he may do poorly or resign on the spot. He does, however, have the ability to write corporate road maps and to design management and operational systems. Planners always make a good staff person, providing appropriate caution. They are usually not feared and are respected for their contribution.

Weaknesses. Planners are not doers and will generally avoid risk taking. They are far more creative than the modifier but will rarely take the risks that a modifier might, even though sold on an idea. For that reason the planner is seldom a good division head or line manager.

CHANGING YOUR STYLE

"The sign of a good book," said Sören Kierkegaard, "is when the book reads you." Hopefully, this chapter is reading you, and you've not only taken a fix on yourself along the two dimensions of risk taking and creativity but you have also examined your own employees in your mind's eye. The nature of your task and the mixture of creative risk takers in your group may well determine your future success.

You may have discovered yourself in a typology you don't like and are asking, "Can I do anything about it?" You can, to an extent, alter your environment to meet your own needs and ideals. You aren't frozen into one life-style. You may be able to alter your work environment. You can surely pick up and try it again in greener pastures. Actually being more creative will also improve with greater risk taking. Try it. Most of us are more creative than we or our organization permits us to be. Sometimes a year away from the job in new circumstances will help. Try a change of life-style or a new vocation. Move out of the community in which you live. All of these actions can contribute to developing your creative sensitivity.

To some degree, you can also change yourself. While you are a product of your genetic and social origins, you still have choices you can make. One way to develop new alternatives is to enter psychotherapy—individual or group. Another is to sate yourself with good management training aimed at attitude change, not just how-to-do-it-better courses. Yet another way is to get involved in sensitivity training in your churches, YMCAs, or company. In other words, deliberately seek involvements where you will have to rethink who you are and what you are about. You need help; you can't do it alone.

Finally, you may like yourself just the way you are. You may see yourself as valuable and not want to cope with the trauma that always attends such personal adjustments. That's not so bad either. You may indeed be making a valuable contribution.

I started by asking if you thought you were uncreative—incapable of coming up with unconventional ideas as a middle manager. I defined risk taking in this light as the ability to tenaciously push those unconventional ideas on top management and your friends at some risk to you. I may have lulled you (for a while) into thinking that I supported the idea that the middle manager can't be creative, that he's locked into a standard mold. You can be creative. You are not locked in.

We talked about eight managerial risk-taking styles, ranging from totally other-directed to totally inner-directed. The chapter goes into some detail about each one, their effect on you and your organization. Where do you fall? Are you happy with the risk taker-creative person that is you? If not, make an effort to change.

UNIT THREE
STRATEGIES FOR REDUCING PERSONAL RISK

THIS UNIT presents some prescriptions for new behavior, but with a twist. The purpose is not to encourage you to take greater risks, although as you learn to get what you want with less actual risk, others will think you to be a greater risk taker. Instead, this unit presents a personal development plan by which your life and work can be more fulfilling and by which you can take more appropriate risks.

Chapter 9 suggests how to time an action so that you get what you want from the organization while minimizing personal loss. How much risk one takes is often related to timing, which many of us don't take into account when we make our plans. Chapter 10 shows how to find out whether your power base allows you to go beyond the explicit authority given you by top management in order to get the job done. Authority is defined, in effect, as the engine, while power is the fuel. One can go as far and as fast as the octane and quality of gas permit.

The title of Chapter 11, "Exercises for Cowards," is, of course, tongue in cheek. We are all cowards to a certain degree. We sometimes equate, unjustifiably, coward-ice with appropriate caution. This chapter suggests to the timorous that you can have fun and develop yourself by doing and thinking some things most of us have been told all of our lives were obnoxious, unchristian, uncivilized, or poor managerial behavior.

Finally, Chapter 12 outlines ways to think and plan about making changes. This chapter prepares you for considering changes in your organization, which is the subject of Unit Four. It also provides a way to look at your personal life and anticipate the potential losses and gains of any proposed change.

9 | When to Take On the Organization

To START an organizational development program of risk management, to use a team approach, or to implement some other innovation that needs top management's support, you better have the right timing. Perhaps the least understood phenomenon of risk taking is when it should be done. Half of life is the right timing. There is a propitious moment to say the truthful thing, to ask for special consideration, or to take a prerogative. Timing is a key concept in risk taking.

We learn—or don't learn—timing when we are young. Mothers teach children not to tell dad about damaging the family car, at least until after supper. Parents teach children not to tell family secrets at the wrong time to the wrong people. Girls wonder when to let that boy kiss them, and boys wonder about the right timing to minimize the chance of rejection. Some people tend to believe that if they get drunk or stoned they'll be forgiven for inappropriate behavior. Bad or good, we learn timing when we are young. Only intensive psychotherapy, sensitivity training, or some other way toward personal growth can really break the pattern of poor timing that some of us have developed.

This chapter won't change your basic behavior pattern, but it will give you a way to examine and evaluate timing that will help you understand why one person's actions produce positive results, while the same behavior in another produces anger and rejection. Obviously, you can't function in your work being constantly concerned about each action or word and possible retribution you may receive for them. Such a practice would cause a preoccupation with risk that would not only lead to a neurosis but would also make you ultraconservative. No, don't begin calculating all of the time.

IDEAL CONDITIONS FOR RISK TAKING
WITHIN THE SYSTEM

Before talking about what risks the middle manager must be prepared to take, let's outline the ideal conditions for risk taking. The following are the conditions that appear to offer the best chance of reducing the actual risk in any interpersonal-organizational situation.

Take risks under the least embarrassing conditions for the other person. In other words, don't grab your boss out on the factory floor and threaten to quit or start raising hell. Don't take risks in front of the boss's boss, a group, or in any other circumstance where you know someone will be embarrassed. Your impertinence may be forgiven, but never your insensitivity. The same applies to how you treat your own subordinates.

Take risks without name calling. Unless you are just ordinarily foul mouthed—and this is accepted as part of your usual style—don't use ad hominem comments to emphasize your point. Calling a person an obscene name can have incalculable effects, compounding your risk many times. Certainly the other person, boss or subordinate, will not take kindly to your idea if it is surrounded by personal insults.

Don't corner the person who has the power and authority. Give these people room. Otherwise, out of feeling pushed, they may respond overharshly, thus vitiating what you really want to have happen, and causing them to respond in a way they would have avoided if possible. When the driver says to the policeman, "Don't give me a lecture, just give me a ticket or let me go," he has foreclosed the options. Twenty to one the guy gets a ticket.

Measure your organization culture for openness. In other words, no matter what the particular risk, a middle manager probably has some built-in limits on how much the organization will tolerate. If your organization is three on a five-point scale of openness, there is some evidence that you can't comfortably go much more than 3.5 and not get rejected. In other words, the very cultural norms determine whether any given risk can be taken profitably.

Don't take risks on paper. When written, anything becomes magnified and distorted far beyond the original intent. Words, even when orally communicated, have power but the associated feelings are like the current of a river—dynamic, momentary, fleeting, and difficult to recapture. Words on paper lose these nuances and the reader must supply his own sense of the writer's feelings. The only time to risk on paper is when it is the only way to get "their" attention. Then be careful to meet the other conditions outlined above.

Don't take risks in social situations. In other words, don't choose the informal setting to deal with the boss. Usually people are the most vulnerable at a social occasion. Some risk takers try to "tell it like it is" from their perspective at that time. The result is usually quite negative. If you do have something to say to the boss, do it on company time.

Don't take risks during a crisis. Confrontations with the organization shouldn't be done when the company has great concern for survival. No president wants to hear, "Either you get me a raise or I'll quit," when profits are so bad that there is no money even for the employee pension fund. This survival mentality does not mean that everyone *should* suddenly become conservative. I'm simply pointing out that, in fact, conservatism is exactly what does happen. Thus, in such a climate, any taking on of the organization, even mildly, is viewed far more dramatically than at other times.

TIMING YOUR RISKS

We discussed the risk of not risking earlier in Chapter 6. Now let's talk about how to time the four major organizational risks the middle manager may have to take to be a good manager.

When to Threaten to Quit

Never threaten to quit unless you mean it and are prepared for the consequences. Your boss will sense how serious you are; if you are bluffing and he calls your bluff, you will lose credibility as well as the only ultimate power you have. Most people don't realize that the possible loss of a valuable employee is always of concern to management. Management may fire but you can quit. Just as you should never threaten an employee, you should never threaten the boss — unless you mean it! It is brinksmanship and can't be carried off without real muscle.

You should threaten to quit when you are asked to violate a serious principle. However, be careful about serious principles and how you define them. No management wants a middle manager who has a principle for every occasion. Define the principles for which you will put your job on the line just like porcupines make love — very carefully. Each person has or should have a first line of oughts and ought-nots. These are usually relative. However, know your second-line, inflexible basic values that supersede any others that may offend them.

A manager must be careful that those principles aren't eroded by small cop-outs requested by superiors or subordinates. He must be able to determine when the first drop of acid is being applied. If, for example, a manager believes he should have pursued openness with supervisors, then he has to be careful about being co-opted by the boss to plot against the supervisors. For example: Boss to middle manager, "Joe, I want to talk to you about Sam and, of course, I don't want you to mention to him that I talked to you." If the middle manager consents, he has been co-opted and his principle has begun to be eroded. We aren't talking here about whether the principle is correct. Rather, the point is how to avoid erosion of principles that lead you finally to say you'll quit over some required action that repulses you but for which you've been set up over the many previous months.

A personnel director of a large government agency was recently faced with the political shenanigans of the Nixon Administration. The new political bosses of Nixon's seasoned team asked him to violate surreptitiously many civil service regulations so that their trusted friends could have key jobs. He faced a matter of principle because, while he constantly compromised those rules in exceptional cases, he was now being told to violate the rules as a general practice. He threatened to quit unless they took the pressure off.

Thus, the only reason you ever threaten to quit is on a matter of principle. Your principles should be few and your self-discipline in avoiding erosion should be constant. Your principle had better be reasonable and you had better be dead serious about it. Finally, as suggested under the rules for risk taking in Chapter 2, don't risk more than you can afford to lose.

When to Confront and Level

Confrontation and leveling are part of the everyday process of being an effective manager. Effective management is based on the manager's ability to give and get adequate information and to make rapid and accurate judgments. Of course, managers come in all sizes and styles. Some are good communicators, some are just shrewd as hell, and others are technically unsurpassed. I suggest, however, that no matter what their strengths, managers can improve their position if they will confront and level, keeping in mind the earlier mentioned criteria.

Confrontation is telling the other person what you think of his actions. It is usually evaluative and usually has some anger associated with it. For example, the marketing director may openly accuse the chief engineer of changing the design for change sake, and point out the various changes, the short intervals between changes, and what he considers to be the lack of significant product improvement. This is confrontation. Of course, the marketing director may simply be angry because he can't sell the new product. Or the chief engineer may not even be responsible for the design changes.

The justice of the accusation isn't being evaluated here. What is important is to understand that such an act is a confrontation and can precipitate getting to the truth behind the circumstances. Such "emotional outbursts" are often held in disfavor by companies. I maintain that emotion expressed under the right conditions, and where the stakes are high, is a perfectly appropriate and often necessary risk to take. Angry emotion is often the best and only opener of a can of organization worms.

Confronting a person is risky, because it tends to carry hostility and threat. When you confront another person, you expose him to judgment or at least put him in a position where he is called upon to respond. You also put yourself in a somewhat vulnerable position because you are acting as prosecutor. But at least during the initial confrontation, you have the upper hand. There is risk for you, but there is more potential risk for the person you confront. Great confronters are often thought of as risk takers in relationships, but the fact is that the person being confronted is in a much riskier situation than the confronter.

If the person being confronted chooses minimal risk, then he responds in one of three ways: confronts in return, complies, or defends himself. The result for you will be the same in all cases: nothing will be solved. No light, just heat. In confronting back, the chief engineer says, "Your salesmen obviously can't sell. If you spent less of your expense money on big parties and more on sales training, you could sell what this company produces. You guys don't want to sell, you just want to be peddlers." The confrontation is mutual and goes nowhere.

The second response may be, "You are right. We'll have to hold those changes down as much as possible." In other words, compliance, but not really. The marketing director will feel better, but next week the same situation will exist.

The third response is defensiveness. The chief engineer will become very feisty, and insultingly explain to the marketing director that, "While you don't understand these changes, we have responded to the market's demands and the design changes forced on us by the competition. If you don't like it, go see the President." Again, we have an impasse.

Any of these impasses might result. All can be temporary if the marketing director will then take the next risk, which is to level. Leveling is telling the other person what his decision or behavior is doing to you. When you level, you share your bind or inadequacy in such a way as to invite the other person to help.

The director of marketing in our case may say, "Look, Tom, let's get it straight. I don't know why the design changes, but I am losing my sales force and having to shift to reps. They are giving me heavy flak because of the design changes. If they are absolutely needed, then I need help in communicating the reasons why." The chief engineer may also then risk leveling by explaining what is really going on. "George, I'm sympathetic, but you may not know that the vice president of engineering is making these decisions. There are mixed feelings in engineering about whether they are necessary. The truth is that you and I shouldn't really be arguing. Your boss and mine should come to an agreement so that we can implement some reasonable approach."

Thus confrontation and leveling are parts of a two-pronged process of continual risk taking that can improve management's communication and problem solving if the organization will tolerate what is sometimes derogatorily referred to as emotionalism.

When to End Run the Boss

Some of us have bosses who can never be circumvented because they are the president or vice president, and enjoy the total confidence of management. An end run under these conditions breaks all three rules of risk taking. However, many middle managers have self-serving bureaucrats as bosses, who simply seek to survive. They make decisions based on their need to survive or to expand their fiefdom at the expense of their subordinates or the goals of the company. With this kind of boss there may come a time when you have to end run.

End runs are dangerous because you violate any potential trust with your boss. The boss will never give you another chance if he loses and you win, or even if he wins and you lose. Thus the stakes must be high and you had better be right. A boss can do many things to keep you from producing or from being seen as effective. He can postpone action on your request in order "to check," "to question," "to change," "to edit," or "to scrutinize more closely." He can hold it, obstruct it, put it in a pigeonhole, or give it back to you.

One middle manager had designed an MBO plan for her entire organization. Her own boss, the director of finance, kept postponing a meeting to review her personal objectives. He broke appointment after appointment for months. He always had something more important to do. Because she could not see him, she could not get his approval to make the plan one of her objectives. Another manager saw his boss override the entire department to install what everyone knew was a poor control system.

Each of these examples cites a middle manager with a dilemma. In each case she or he must apply the three rules of risk taking: consider the odds, don't risk a lot for a little, and don't risk more than you can afford to lose. Once satisfied that these criteria have been met, end run the boss if necessary. That's good management.

Of course, the more satisfactory situation is provided by a team approach or by a more participative organization, as we will discuss in Unit Four. Under such a system the pros and cons would have been openly discussed, and the chances of having to end run the boss would be lessened because he would have probably been more open to influence and would also have had the opportunity to air his own views. But most companies don't operate so openly, which means you may have to take the personal risk on an occasion to protect either the company or yourself.

When to Hold Out

Holding out means becoming immobile, unyielding, uncooperative, stubborn, recalcitrant, mule headed—in other words, impossible. Sometimes that is all the force a middle manager can bring to bear. His dead weight may prevent a decision being made, a wrong policy being instituted, or a valuable employee being fired. Holding out is a deliberate form of work slowdown, insubordination, and disobedience. It is risky, but under some conditions it is a necessary risk.

In my company we had an opportunity to form an association with a well-known professional colleague. The entire team felt positively inclined, except for one person. She said no. During the month or so of discussions, this one person was badgered to change her position. She was accused of self-serving motivations. Over and over she had to try to explain why, intuitively, she was opposed to the association. No amount of persuasion seemed to move her. Finally, factors began to emerge that seemed to support the lack of fit she had suspected but had not been able to explain. The company subsequently cut off negotiations with the person, and months later everyone was relieved. But she took the risk. She took the punishment meted out to the holdouts in organizations.

In the Bay of Pigs incident, Kennedy asked, "How could we have been so stupid?" Irving L. Janis suggests the problem was not intelligence but groupthink, what he calls the deterioration in mental efficiency, reality testing, and moral judgment as a result of group pressure.[1] An associated phenomenon with the same results is what Jerry Harvey calls the Abilene paradox.[2] Apparently many felt the decision to invade Cuba was excessively risky, but there were no holdouts. No one was willing to risk being the one to buck the tide, to question the majority, to hold out against all costs. There was a collusion against the truth. One holdout could have prevented that infamous day.

In organizations that use consensus or concurrence-seeking methods, there is a danger that a cohesive in-group will tend to override realistic appraisal of alternative courses of action. The middle manager can either encourage the dissenter or be the holdout himself when appropriate. In a memo to his colleagues, one manager, installing a team approach in his research organization, noted some important issues regarding the fear of groupiness and the use of holdouts. Here are excerpts from the memo:

> Group cohesiveness tends to grow in team development. Cohesiveness in my opinion is no virtue, if it leads to suppression of criticality. Mutual support to encourage disclosure of "where you are" on an issue will bring out the "deviant" thoughts. As I write this, it sounds like I'm encouraging chaos, but my experience is that groups that interact in this way move more quickly to consensus than groups where the characteristic stance is guarded. Boss dominated groups move quickly to the decisions the boss requests, but any consensus reached in this way is coincidental.
>
> Some of you have expressed to me your apprehension of "groupthink." My comments are that team development does not necessarily lead to groupthink, though aspects of groupthink are potential traps. Why then team development? The *creative contributions* come from individuals, but good group interaction can open the horizons of the individual. The challenge of disagreement and conflict in the team can promote creativity. Team development helps you to manage conflict, not to suppress it. A good team draws out its silent partners and gets their inputs into the thinking. Individuals usually feel more ownership of a decision if it's been fought out in team process. *We have to work in groups* to do our job. Team development is for the purpose of working more effectively.[3]

Of course, an organization such as that advocated by Sackett lowers the risk for the person who is divergent, who holds out.

Most organizations still require the individual to take his lumps for unpopular positions when he believes he's right. So just be right!

In this chapter we discussed the seven conditions that affect any major risks a middle manager might wish to take. Timing, of course, is the name of the game, whether it is in a gambling casino or in corporate politics. Given the fact that these seven factors affect the timing of any confrontation of the organization, what are the major risks and their attendant conditons? The first is, "When do you threaten to quit?" The ideal answer is when a primary principle is being violated, but don't draw your gun unless you intend to use it. The second is, "When do you confront and level?" The obvious answer is that it is a great style of life when the organizational climate is prepared for "emotionalism," especially the boss. The third is, "When do you end run the boss?" Only when the stakes are high, either for yourself or for the company. The fourth risk is, "When do you hold out?" The answer we explored was when you really believe you are right. Numbers of opposing people should never be a consideration when you think you are right.

10 | Going Beyond Expectations

WHEN MANAGERS, faced with a difficult task, disclaim their responsibility with evasions like, "I haven't got the authority to do that" or "I can't take the risk," they usually mean that they lack an extrinsic symbol—a job description or a job title—to authorize them to make that move. Looking for power in these tangibles, however, prevents them from seeing the intangible source of their real power: the respect of their boss and their peers and the self-esteem that comes from being professionals committed to their own goals as well as to the goals of the organization.

Taking personal risks, which means moving beyond the expectations of peers and the boss, can be a successful venture for a manager as long as the risk taking is securely grounded in power and authority. These two factors, however, are not identical. And a manager who plans on reaping the benefits of risk taking needs to understand how power and authority operate in an organization.

AUTHORITY

There is a difference between power and authority as I use these concepts. Authority is defined here as the sanction a manager needs to perform certain supervisory functions, make decisions, or commit the organization to some future course. Authority always deals with what is expected. The policeman has the authority to arrest you, but not to try and hang you. As a parent, the state gives you authority over the behavior of an underage child. Once the child becomes of age, you no longer have that authority. The advertising manager has no authority in the art director's department.

Sometimes there is confusion. Does, for example, the vice president to whom both the advertising manager and the art director report have authority in their departments? Does the police chief have authority to intervene in an arrest being performed by a sergeant? In other words, although most of us seek to have clear authority, it is always relative and almost always unclear. This fact of organizational life is least clear to middle managers whose authority is almost always unclear. One reason it is unclear is that life doesn't fit into job descriptions. Top management may say, "You are in charge of the layout department." The actual state of being in charge has to be worked out on a daily basis among the people involved.

Let's go back to the policeman illustration. If, in fact, the policeman isn't to try me but only to apprehend, then why does he give me a lecture? Perhaps the policeman may make a judgment that the circumstances around my obviously having broken the law were so mitigating that he will let me off. Isn't he trying and sentencing me? Of course he is, and, within limits, society wants that to happen. Within limits, top management wants middle management to exceed its formal authority because there is no way that authority can be given to cover every situation.

Let's talk about authority in a company. There are three kinds. The first is that authority granted by the designated management that represents the owner. In our capitalist society the owner may be an entrepreneur or group of entrepreneurs, a publicly owned company with professional management, or a cooperative. In all cases management represents the owners, and their authority is derived from the owners. Thus all delegated authority essentially belongs to the owners. Presumably, the owners can take back authority from management any time within whatever legal restraints exist. Most often, if management isn't successful it is replaced over a period of time.

The second kind of authority is that which is given by peers.

For example, shop stewards or union representatives, elected by their colleagues, are authorized by a constituency other than management to act for employees in the same organization. With the increase of professional associations and managerial unions, middle management in the future may be operating out of two opposing authority bases. On the one hand, they'll be asked to represent the interests of top management to their subordinates. On the other, they'll have to represent their own interests. Owner-delegated and peer-derived authority may produce paralyzing conflict in the middle manager ranks.

The third kind of authority is that derived from oneself. It is the personal authority of persons who set their own values and then act on them to whatever extent needed. It is the authority of the person in a movie theater who assumes command in a panic resulting from a fire. It is that of the town sanitarian who tells the builder that the proposed building must have the ventilator that is more expensive but better than the building code requires. The builder, naturally angry, threatens to take it to the courts. The sanitarian urges him to go ahead and sue. He'll have to pay court costs and lose the time. The builder is caught because it is less expensive to simply conform. Does the sanitarian have the authority? No; not from an external base other than himself. The same authority was recognized in Jesus when he preached in the temple. It was said that he spoke with authority, not as the scribes and Pharisees. He was his own authorizing body. So many people, often the most successful, are totally unauthorized by any force outside themselves. A commanding voice, a strong ego, and a sense of one's rightness can overcome many conventional obstacles.

Each of these bases for acting is increasingly risky. To act on management's authority may be risky because you may not have top management's backing in an actual crunch. Acting on peer authority is risky because if top management resents your action, it may get you later. Your colleagues' support may vanish in a showdown. Of course, the authority base that makes managers most vulnerable is that of themselves. See Figure 5 for an illustration of the increasing risks.

When middle managers claim no authority to perform an independent act of judgment beyond their management base, they

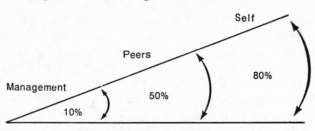

Figure 5.   Risk arc.

are avoiding greater risk. When they say, "I'll do it, although it may be my neck," they are simply recognizing that they are on their own and the corporate risks are greater for their personal careers.

POWER

You are probably accusing me of oversimplifying, and I am. So at this point, let's start to tie everything together by talking about power. My definition of power in an organization is relatively discrete from authority. Power isn't job descriptions, high positions in the hierarchy, or self-authorized decisions. Power is what permits one manager to continuously exceed boundaries and expectations with occasional buffetings from top management but with overall praise. Some managers get in trouble when they overstay their lunch hour fifteen minutes. Power is the factor that makes the difference. It adds to your authority—whether that authority derives from management, your peer group, or yourself.

Power is the ability to control the behavior of other people. Authority gives you the legal right but power is the muscle. The president has the authority to keep the railroads running despite a proposed strike, but the army runs the railroad. They have power. The U.S. Supreme Court has the authority to order a school to comply with desegregation requirements. But if there were no U.S. marshals to enforce the compliance, the authority would be meaningless. I have the authority to tell my son when to come home. He comes home because of my power, not my authority.

From our discussion so far, you may think that power is only a matter of coercion. However, there are many other bases for power: friendships, personal traits, self-confidence, opportunity, information, expertise, status, seniority, connections, proprietorship, interpersonal skills. All of these factors are additive power factors that the possessor uses as the basis of action to be a mover and doer. Women understand power better than most men, for having been consistently discriminated against in receiving authority within the culture, they have learned uses of power unknown by men, including sexual exploitation or, at least, the use of sexual wiles. I don't frown on this, for one uses whatever power one has, especially when disenfranchised by a dominant majority.

Risk taking, then, is a function of both authority and power. The more power one has, the less risk there is in exceeding management or peer expectations, that is, in acting on one's own authority. Without power, any kind of authority is to no avail; with power, any kind of authority has less risk attached. Thus managers who are interested in deriving the benefits from creative risk taking must examine and exploit the sources of their power.

Friendship

The network of a manager's social relations within the organization is a prime source of power. Such power works from two directions: vertical and horizontal. An illustration of vertical friendship is the manager who is always invited to the president's Christmas parties or out for weekends. As a result, this relationship may intimidate the manager's peers into granting her a great deal of power. Although the president may be unaware of the effect of the association with a subordinate, the subordinate is rarely unaware of its important boost to her power level. She may even presume upon her relationship with the president during team meetings to get her point across.

The power of vertical friendship is not limited to social relationships. In one toy and game development company, for example, the values, tastes, and general attitudes of the president and one member of the creative team obviously had more affinity than those of other team members. The result of this rapport was that, whether justified or not, the team members credited their peer with an excessive amount of influence on the team's decision making.

On the horizontal level, a manager can develop strong friendships through country clubs, board meetings of other companies, and management training courses with key people in other divisions or departments. She can get what she wants done in the organization because she knows on whom to call. Even in the largest organizations, friendship holds weight in the informal influence system.

Desirable Personal Traits

Whether a manager has the personality traits most valued by his employees, peers, and boss depends on the situation. "One man's meat is another man's poison" is a cliché that applies here. A sales department may greatly admire the tough battler who supports his people and fights for their mutual interests. The engineering department, on the other hand, may consider intelligence and coolness under fire, rather than warmth, the best qualities of a chief engineer. There is no clear set of desirable traits in a manager except those that are appreciated by the corporation's management and by the manager's peers and subordinates. Nurturing traits that are attractive, nevertheless, creates a base of power that allows a manager to act more autonomously in an organization.

A striking example of the influence of personal traits was shown when 20 managers of a manufacturing company were signing in at a hotel for a management conference, and were given the option of whom they would like for a roommate. Sixteen chose one young manager who was almost unknown to top management at that time. It was discovered that this man's personal traits were so attractive to this group of hard-nosed manufacturing personnel that all wished to be his roommate. This created for the young manager another base of power within the organization that would allow him to act more autonomously.

Opportunity

To state the obvious, one of the reasons we marry the people we do is because they were the ones we knew. Often we were brought up in the same neighborhood. We had the opportunity to get to know each other better than some other people. The same kind of opportunity allows some people within the organization to have more influence than others.

A simple factor like office location can be a source of power. Sometimes it is as simple as whether you work on the right floor of the building where the action is, or whether you have a favorable boss who sends you to meetings in his place. Many people are not sensitive to the opportunities resulting from having an office on the same floor as the president's. A casual morning hello, or a special personal interest by the boss in your project, gives you an opportunity to be in touch with him more frequently than other project managers. Even the fact that your secretary is a close friend of the secretary to the president or to another decision maker can give you opportunities that others do not have. The vice president of sales in a subsidiary far away from the home office has fewer opportunities to build an informal relationship with the chief executive than does the vice president of a subsidiary in the same town as the home office.

Perceived Expertise

Another key source of power in an organization is how expert a manager is thought to be by management and by his fellow workers. In one company, the chief engineer was known not only as the oracle but also as the person who had to approve new ideas. He had a reputation for demanding quality engineering and homework, even from the sales department. Based on his perceived competence, this manager had final veto over any new product. In an insurance firm dealing with casualty claims, the man responsible for investigating and making recommendations related to loss, if he is highly knowledgeable and competent, can command great influence in deciding who next year's customers will be.

Information

"In 1948 we tried that and thus and thus happened." Being able to describe what has happened in the past gives a person weight in decision making. Furthermore, managers who develop for themselves continuing education programs and become sources of information in decision making increase their influence.

Regardless of the kind of knowledge the manager has—whether it be the ins and outs of management by objectives, new mass marketing techniques, or the science-based program of organizational development—this knowledge bestows upon him personal power.

Personal Confidence

One trait that underscores a manager's influence is the degree of self-confidence he feels and communicates to others. Admitting mistakes is the fastest way managers can persuade subordinates to trust their judgment. A good example of the attitude of a confident manager who has self-esteem is described by Robert Townsend in *Up the Organization:*

> Admit your own mistakes openly, maybe even joyfully. . . . My batting average on decisions at Avis was no better than .333. Two out of every three decisions I made were wrong. But my mistakes were discussed openly and most of them corrected with a little help from my friends.[1]

One manager walked into his boss's office, really fuming. He was angry as hell. He said to himself, "No matter what happens, I'm going to tell her she can't do that anymore." He said, when he returned, "Well, I told her, and while telling her, I was quite emotional. She floored me when she responded by saying, 'I agree with you and I won't do that again.'"

These are both examples of personal confidence that gains the trust of your people and creates another power base for you.

Status

Are you a president or a tool-and-diemaker apprentice? No matter how many writers, such as Robert Townsend, or organizations, such as Texas Instruments, try to strip organizations of the falderal and bric-a-brac that goes with different kinds of status within the organization, status still is an important factor. Rugs on office floors, names on parking places in the parking lot, credenzas, titles—all stress the importance of status within the organization. It is still quite possible to lure a bright young man away from another company with the promise of his becoming an officer in the new company, even though the salary may be no greater and, in fact, may be smaller. Being vice president in a bank is of very little consequence financially, but the accompanying status is a very important factor in the lives of many bankers. Therefore, in calculating your influence in the organization, you need to assess the effect of your status on other personnel.

Seniority

The length of time you have served the organization will affect how your peers, subordinates, and superiors view your potential. The influence of seniority is no longer as important as it once was. However, what might be called survival rate of a manager during periods of upheaval (which broadly can be interpreted as seniority) does definitely increase his influence within the organization. For example, a great deal of influence is attributed to a controller by his peers if he has managed to survive three presidents in two years. The fact that the controller is that valuable to the company makes them quite wary of crossing his wishes in any way. Such influence might never be explicitly discussed or accepted, but the effect is obvious to the outside observer.

The effects of this kind of influence often are seen in the way information is pipelined to the president. For example, if the controller says that certain new equipment cannot be purchased because it is too expensive, department heads with less seniority may not question her decision, even though it is simply a matter of the controller's opinion rather than a policy statement by the president. It has been my experience that when a controller has this kind of influence, she can turn down normal requests for raises and compensation, maintenance costs, expense accounts, and many other day-to-day necessities, leaving the manager apparently no recourse.

Interpersonal Skills

The ways in which you are able to work effectively with others add to your power. The manager who has interpersonal skills gains great impact when they are added to other kinds of power bases. Interpersonal skills by this definition include effective listening, effective communication, clarity of thoughts, empathy in relationships, and so on. A manager who consistently finds his intentions misread by co-workers most probably lacks interpersonal skills. On the other hand, the manager whose intentions are generally perceived in the same way as his behavior has very influential interpersonal skills.

Real interpersonal skill is being able to communicate and be understood accurately and to form meaningful relationships with the people with whom you work. To the degree to which you can form those relationships and are accurately perceived by others, you increase your managerial influence within the organization.

The manager who tells his employee something about another manager and asks him not to tell the other manager tends to be divisive, and creates mystery and in-group, out-group kinds of relationships. This kind of a manager, although skilled in many other areas, will not gain influence through interpersonal effectiveness. The manager who punishes his employees verbally without being sensitive to the situation may also lack the influence that comes from effective interpersonal skills. Many of us do not really know how much interpersonal skill we have because we have so little feedback from others. However, one test is, "How much do you feel you are misunderstood by those with whom you work?" To that degree your skills are limited.

In order to gain influence in an organization, you need to multiply your bases of power, for the greater number of power sources you have, the less risk it is to *take* authority when desirable. Look, then, at Figure 6, which describes the relationship between the multiple power bases and the different kinds of authority in the organization. Place a 0, 1, 2, or 3 in each box to indicate little (0) or much (3) of a particular type of power you think you have in the organization.

After placing the appropriate number in each box, you may wish to take into account the difference in magnitude between power factors. In some companies any power factor may have a greater significance than allowed for in the diagram. In order to account for that factor, simply multiply the score you give yourself on any particular power factor by the magnitude you feel that variable has within your company. For example, if you've given yourself 3 on personal confidence, and in your judgment it is twice as important as other factors, then when you sum up your total power factor, give personal confidence a 6.

If you have no more than a 9-point total power base, you will be taking personal risk when you go beyond your delegated authorization. If you have no more than an 18-point total, you can go beyond your delegated authority with peer support with little personal risk. The closer to a 27-point total you have, the greater the possibility that you can make many self-authorized decisions with little organizational disapproval.

In other words, personal risk in taking authority is directly related to the power base you hold; therefore it is relative. Thus, for example, when a group of middle managers refuses to take authority, it is probably because they feel they do not have more

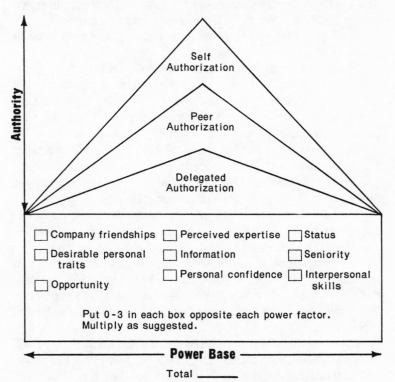

Figure 6.   Power and authority pyramid.

than a 9-point power base to move from. On the other hand, if a general manager of a company walks through the plant and changes procedures as he sees fit, he thinks of himself with a 28-point power base. In neither case is there personal risk.

To be a creative risk-taking manager in your organization you must assess your power base accurately and take a little more authority than your power base allows when it is necessary to get the job done. This does not mean, however, that you have license to act as a self-authorizing employee at all times. That is compulsive rather than creative risk.

Chapter 10 dealt with power and authority as they affect the risk-taking behavior of the middle manager. Authority is defined as the official sanction a manager needs to perform certain supervisory functions. Power is the ability to control the behavior of other people. These are interrelated concepts, and both must be understood as part of taking a risk.

Middle managers have three sources of authority: from designated management, from peers, and from themselves. The amount of risk attached to each varies, with the least risk from acting out of authority derived from management and the most from acting out of personal, or internally derived, authority. We discussed nine sources of power available to the middle manager. Each may have a different value in your organization. Certainly you do not possess each of them to the same degree, nor are you limited only to those sources of power mentioned.

The idea is to assess realistically the quantity and quality of the power and authority you have, and then go on from there. Do you have the authority to make major, or even minor, changes in your organization? If not, how far do you have to stretch your existing authority base? If you do have the authority, do you have the power, the muscle, to enforce your decisions? Do you understand the sources of your power, how to use them, and how to increase them?

If you want to be a creative risk-taking manager you will have to put some time and energy into this assessment of power and authority. You will have to figure out just how much you have, how much you want, and how much of a risk you take each time you want to exceed your own personal margin of safety.

11 | Exercises for Cowards

This CHAPTER is not for the cocky, the aggressive, or the decisive. Rather, it is for those who feel cut off at the pass. There are thousands of you: You try to listen to other people's problems, you look out first for the company's interest, and you are often pushed around by smart-aleck bosses or associates who seem primarily to be thinking about number one. My guess is that you are over 30 and are regarded as a valuable piece of equipment — predictable, loyal, inarticulate, and generally not a troublemaker. This chapter is for you.

In this chapter I suggest some exercises that will develop that other side of yourself, not to make you obnoxious and self-seeking, but rather to guide you toward a synthesis of the polarities of every dimension of life. These exercises are similar to isometrics. They are a way to push against your current psychic muscles, a way to quietly work out with new behavior. If you are not prepared to try some behavior that is "not you," then skip this chapter.

Most management courses emphasize skills that you probably are already pretty good at. IBM wants to teach you listening skills. AMA wants you to become a better planner. Human relations courses want you to relate more effectively, warmly, and empathetically to others. Of course it is important to develop these skills, which are in constant need of improvement. But it's even more important that middle managers become more aggressive, demanding, provocative, and troublesome, not more compliant, warm, and understanding.

Few management courses offer such training. The closest to it may be Dale Carnegie's *How to Win Friends and Influence People* and, although quite dissimilar in method and learning theory, the Creative Risk Taking workshop (see appendix). Nobody thinks of helping you to fight rather than to love, to stick up for yourself rather than to stick up for everyone else. Nice guys often finish last, and too often that's exactly what middle managers are — nice guys.

Of course, no one wants non-nice guys, but there must be a synthesis of the two that most of us can achieve if our spouses, friends, top management, and enemies will permit it. They often have a big stake in our remaining the same, easy-to-get-along-with, good-tempered person. Eagle scouts have their place, but very often they march in it until they drop. Don't let your need to be liked and your fear of failure chain you down.

Management courses tend to reinforce all those values about how good it is to be unassuming and cooperative, while the big shots who send you to these courses are cocky, bossy, and tough. My contention is that the cocky, bossy, tough person makes a better team player than the passive, altruistic middle manager. Tough people are assertive — they say what they want and put their cards on the table from the beginning.

EXERCISES FOR GROWTH

Many of us have been carefully coached into being emotional and spiritual dwarfs by teachers who didn't want trouble; parents who didn't want us to reflect badly on them; and clergymen who were sure you had to crawl into the Kingdom of Heaven to be worthy. In order for the dwarf in us to grow, we must consciously do things that shape us in a different way. Like children, we must pretend to be what we want until we actually are more like what we pretend to be. Our emotions can expand, but we need to have large enough self-concepts for them to fill the space. As long as you view yourself as an emotional dwarf, you'll not grow taller emotionally. An exercise can help grow the new limb you want.

It is, however, only an exercise, and should not lead you to a life of pretense any more than it does a five-year-old who plays cowboy all the time. But just as a child may become more mature as a result of playing a role, you may discover unknown strengths by playing new roles temporarily.

These exercises, then, involve doing something to someone else that you wouldn't ordinarily do; saying something to someone else you wouldn't ordinarily say. It can be done with someone who knows you, such as your spouse or your boss. It may be someone who has never met you before—a delivery boy or a busdriver—and who therefore has no expectations for you to violate. In each case you will be "trying on" behavior that would cause people who knew you to say "That's not like George. He's never been like that."

The exercises themselves will be exaggerated and feel uncomfortable. The thing to remember is that an exercise is always exaggerated in order to build the muscle. When I lift weights I always lift more than I would normally lift of furniture or other objects. I never do situps in quite the same way I actually sit up. In other words, an exercise is exactly that—an exercise. It leads to increased capacity. The exercise itself is not suggested as a way of life.

All right, let's get on with the five basic exercises:

The immaculate perceiver
Stop talking to yourself
Be a prodigal son
Be a lousy listener
That's your problem

For each exercise, I will suggest how to do it, with whom, and when. You will have to decide whether you agree, and then pick your own times, places, and people.

The Immaculate Perceiver

When you constantly feel doubt, you hedge your observations. You say, "I think that new account may be in trouble." Your cocky associate will say, "No, George, I checked. It's A-OK." You may still feel on edge but, being a "nice guy," you put your fears away. Three weeks later you are vindicated because, indeed, the account was in trouble. The difficulty is that no one knew that you had had those early doubts. Your fast-talking friend, however, is now telling top management how he had anticipated the problems and why the fault lay with the account, not with him.

You feel that everyone except you seems to really understand what's going on—in politics (*Let me tell you what Nixon's really doing . . .*), in religion (*The one true and only way to salvation is . . .*), in sales projection (*We'll crack three million, no doubt about it . . .*), in personal relationships (*I like people and people like me . . .*). Other people seem to lack the edge of doubt that makes you hedge every opinion and observation. People's faces, their set jaws, and knowing looks surprise you because you don't have that much confidence in your observational powers. The fact that you are often proved right (to yourself) later doesn't give you confidence for the next time someone turns to you and says, "OK, George, give me a guaranteed delivery date." You still hedge and feel a lack of self-confidence.

If what I've said describes you, then you might try the immaculate perceiver exercise. In this exercise, no matter how you really feel, you suspend your feelings and make an assumption that your doubts are wrong and, in fact, that you have the *only* correct view. In application it means you respond to the boss with, "Count on delivery in 30 days." If you feel it might actually be sooner or later don't communicate that. Thirty days is your best and only judgment for now. If anyone challenges you, don't get involved. "OK, Tom, you're entitled to your opinion, but I know what I'm talking about." Very likely Tom will then back down, intimidated by the sureness in your voice. Of course you may be slightly wrong, but that can be compensated for unless you are totally out of the ballpark on your estimates. Remember, I'm not suggesting that you lie or distort the facts. I'm only saying, don't create doubt. Give the facts, or an educated guess, but do it with confidence.

Immaculate perception can be practiced with your wife. She: "George, do you think the play will be worth spending a whole evening with the Johnsons?" George: "You bet!" No hedging. No taking it back. So what if it doesn't turn out well? You won't be held responsible.

Immaculate perception can also help a group. Let's say that a decision is about to be made to buy a piece of expensive equipment that you are certain will be a waste of money. Everyone else seems to feel that it will be the answer to production problems. Ordinarily, the 20 percent doubt you have about your judgment will make you say to yourself, "Well, George, you could be wrong. They seem to be so sure."

But let's assume that you are practicing immaculate perception. You therefore say (not to yourself as you usually do, but to the group), "There is no way I'll agree to the purchase. It's a waste of money, so forget it." Your absolute conviction will provoke more conversation and examination of the odds of success. Almost certainly, others will begin sharing doubts that they had not previously expressed. If the decision is still made to buy the equipment, you will have had your say, more factors will have been considered, and perhaps a better decision will have been made. If the purchase proves to be foolish, you'll be a hero.

Immaculate perception simply means voicing an opinion that you hold to be 70 percent true in a 100 percent tone of voice. It can be practiced with everyone, all the time. Sometimes the power of that extra 30 percent will even make you laugh to yourself, for you won't believe it at first and maybe you never will. But you will find that in dealing with 100 percent conviction, the cockiest subordinate, associate, or boss hesitates before overruling or undercutting what you think is right.

The risk is low. If you are wrong, people will say, "George may not always be right, but you know what he thinks." If you are right, people will say, "By God, that George is right again." Try the immaculate perception exercise and see the difference it will make with how seriously you are taken.

Stop Talking to Yourself

Perhaps the middle manager's worst habit is talking to himself. After being put down in a meeting, the middle manager says to himself, "That son of a bitch. Who gives him the right to talk to me like that? I'd like to get him out on the handball court and give him a couple of good body blocks. Anyway, he can't even run his own life much less this company—divorced, kids on dope. . . ." On and on go the vindictive feelings internally expressed. The self-justifying language is really a form of rebuilding one's ego after being bested by another person. The anger is really directed at yourself, because it is only expressed internally and you are the only person at the receiving end. To paraphrase, "He apparently has the right to talk to me that way. I let him do it. I'm afraid to give him verbal licks. I can't really run my own life."

Or, during meetings, he says to himself, "That guy drones on and on. How long will this damn meeting last? I've got to get those calls in before lunch." About the secretary who sits on the corner of his desk, he thinks, "Who told this woman she could sit on my desk? I get so tired of these fresh kids. None of them were brought up right." On and on go the private conversations, sometimes about extremely important matters and at other times about small but abrasive events. The other person has little inkling that behind your blank stare are baleful, angry, or even sometimes loving thoughts. He sees you as Mr. Nice Guy who can be pushed around and doesn't mind.

Of course you hold back because you are afraid of the consequences. You are afraid that if you say those things to your boss in that meeting she will fire you. You think that if you say you'd like to leave a meeting to make phone calls and that the meeting is a waste of time anyway, you'll offend people permanently. You "know" that you'll have a hard time getting work out of the secretary if you tell her what you think. On all counts you are probably right. If, in fact, you let loose your stream of invectives on any of these people they'd be discomfited—"That's not like George"—and you'll be embarrassed, if not fired.

But you don't have to sit on your feelings and stockpile all your angry moments. The usual result of such action is that you simply transfer your negative feelings to another person who has less power to hurt you. For example, instead of thinking the thoughts about the boss, you can say immediately, "Excuse me, Ms. Jones, you misunderstood me," or "I wasn't through when you interrupted," or "Please let me complete the idea I had started." In other words, don't let it fester inside you. Deal immediately with the feeling of being put down by getting back up. Most people won't even know you got knocked down, you've let it happen so often. The boss probably took a fix on you some time ago and figured you for Harpo Marx. She's not even aware that she just shoved you in the mud. You've got to say to your head (when you start talking to yourself), "Stop! Talk out loud. Say anything but don't talk to yourself, George. Don't hate yourself."

The dull meeting can be easily dealt with, too. If you feel 70 percent sure that the meeting is dull or unnecessary, say so before you build up a head of steam that sears your insides or that you let out in the bathroom with another fearful associate who'll commiserate with you. I find that if I feel a meeting is poor, the odds are strong that others feel the same. Bet on the come and say *right away,* "Is this meeting really necessary?" or "Can we set a time limit on this meeting?" or, if you are willing to take a bit more flak, "I'm really beginning not to listen and would like to knock off this meeting." Again, there is less risk than you think. If others don't feel the same way as you, they will at least have to deal with your needs in order to have a productive meeting. They will value your time more. If they do agree with you, you'll be considered influential and helpful.

The secretary is a bit more difficult to cope with. You have already convinced her, by not being direct before, that you are an old shoe, and nothing gets treated more casually than an old shoe. At least offer her a chair in lieu of the desk. In any case, you must not talk to yourself. If the chair isn't a good idea, risk telling her, "You know, Mary, I enjoy our relationship but I don't like to be considered an old shoe, and when you sit on my desk that's the way I feel." Don't expect her to love you for this. She may respect you more but she may not speak for a few days. In other words, stockpiled feelings are inappropriate when they are finally expressed, and often such blowups astonish the person you are offended by. On the other hand, if you express your feelings at the time they are aroused, you will probably only bruise the other person.

What do you do with those tender, loving feelings that you often talk to yourself about? That's a tough one, because the emotions related to love are often more difficult to express and their impact harder to control than those related to anger. Sometimes the best intentions are perceived as a pass by a person of the opposite sex. I'm old-fashioned enough not to want those kinds of involvements. You may be different. In a business world where women and men increasingly associate and where homosexual love receives more acceptance, there is greater potential for love-sex involvements in the office. Sometimes getting the subject out on the table with the potential problem person early will clear the air. At other times it will be destructive. As far as the business goes, if you are daydreaming about all the women or men in the office, you'd better stop talking to yourself. Talk to the person, your spouse, a friend, but don't just talk to yourself.

I am proposing that you act and talk more to others when you are tempted to talk to yourself. Try it with the waiter who treats you like a second-class citizen. Try it in the boardroom during operations meetings. There's little risk and lots of return on the investment.

Be a Prodigal Son

Some people are more oriented toward meeting the demands of others rather than demanding from others. We are taught early in life not to say, "I want," "I need," "it's mine." Children are very demanding, and most parents teach their children that such behavior is unacceptable, that they must learn to couch their needs and demands in unabrasive terms. The social graces aren't all bad, and may help ease a tight situation. Anyway, everyone soon learns to read the code. The difficulty often lies in speaking the plain truth.

For some of us, the legitimate feelings of "I want," "I need," "it's mine" actually get destroyed and such expressions are no longer in our vocabulary. We have been consciously dead to our needs for years. Thus we often express our needs very covertly, even hiding them from ourselves. Perhaps you'll rediscover them through your sense of injustice when an obviously self-seeking colleague gets promoted while others, including you, who are self-effacing, are still waiting. The promoted manager seems to be selfish, self-centered, and attention-getting, while the faithful, who think of others and are company-centered team players, get stepped on.

The truth of it is that all of us need some internal synthesis of the self-seeking, narcissistic, demanding, prodigal part of ourselves and the faithful, predictable, helpful, altruistic part. Neither side in itself is very attractive. Make more demands at work. Be the highest paid in your rank. Squeak until greased. Demand the office you think can best help you do your job. Try getting the help of the best secretary and demand that your work be done on time. Expect and demand your subordinates' work to be letter-perfect, because it reflects on you.

Expect first-class treatment at your hotel. Demand your money back when you are treated sloppily. Demand the least expensive but best of everything. When you eat out, pay only for excellent food and service. Don't hesitate to leave a restaurant when the menu, the environment, or the service is inadequate. Quit making allowances for people when they don't shape up. You aren't helping anyone by letting him become slipshod, and you certainly aren't getting what you deserve.

Now you may be saying, "I can't do that. That's obnoxious, unchristian, and anyway I can't bring it off." Well, you can in little ways, and you will never appear as brazen to others as you will to yourself. If you are a sales person, practice being more forward and less ingratiating. You've got a good product. If you haven't, then sell something else. Let the customers know that you are doing them a favor. Don't let the garage man intimidate you. If he doesn't fix your car, don't just boycott him. Demand that he take care of you.

In other words, get in touch with the prodigal in you. The world has forces that are not going to like your demands. All those associates with need-suppressing mothers and fathers are going to reprimand and think badly of you. Top management may have to get angry and then forgive you more often, but they'll respect you if the result is a synthesis within you of prodigal and "older son."

Be a Lousy Listener

"One of Tom's greatest attributes is that he is a good listener." This statement can mean that Tom is a person who hears not only the content but the intent of the speaker. That's a good listener. But what it probably means is that I can corner Tom and he'll listen to anything for as long as I want him to.

Many a management meeting is held where a vice president or president talks to middle managers for hours at a time while they appear to listen politely. Cocktail parties are ideal places for an attractive female manager to get trapped by inebriated bosses or colleagues who fancy themselves as exciting conversationalists.

In all these cases, you probably aren't listening; you just look like it. That makes you easy prey for talkers who use your time without really taking into consideration how you want to use your time. Practice becoming a lousy listener.

1. *Never listen unless you've made an agreement with the speaker for how long the conversation will last.* You can't discipline yourself so it's best to set ground rules early. Just say, "Sure, Sam, I've got about 15 minutes. Is that enough time?" Sam will usually say yes.

2. *Try trading experiences.* Suppose the speaker is telling you about how sick the dog is or how the ballgame turned out. Wait for an opening and tell him about your son's white rat and its bad habits and about your new television set. In other words, don't ask for more information. Just match story for story.

3. *Don't listen to excuses.* When subordinates start explaining why they are late, or why they didn't do what they said they would, cut them off. Tell them you don't want to hear it. They were late and there isn't anything else to say. Perhaps you appear to be more understanding than you really are by pretending to be a good listener. Tell them you don't want to listen. You just want them to be on time. They will call you a lousy listener.

4. *Try the domino approach.* The domino approach is very simple. When other people are talking and you are bored, wait until they are finished. Respond briefly to what they've just said and then change the subject to something you want to talk about. For example, a colleague is telling you at length why she and her husband are buying a house in a particular neighborhood. She goes on for some time and you are giving her your usual "I am listening very actively" look. You suddenly become aware of what you are doing. Wait until there is an opening. She—"Yes, well the curbs and gutters are new but we have to pay exorbitant assessments." You—"Assessments are a problem. They seem so unfair. You know, someone just decides for you. *Which re-*

minds me, did you and the others happen to decide that I should go to that marketing meeting next week? I understand someone committed me to go."

5. *Drift your eyeballs.* Look at your watch. While the other person is talking, try letting your eyeballs drift to either side of him, vacantly looking away, or take a quick look at your watch. The other person will soon get the idea that the time is up, or at least that he needs to regain your attention.

Yes, I'm seriously suggesting that the chief problem for many middle managers is that they give the appearance of and often actually do listen too much. Being an effective manager means to share in the give-and-take among colleagues, subordinates, and bosses, and to be selective about use of time. You, not others, should decide how to use your time. True management is learning how to become a lousy listener. Consistently having a listening posture will give you a reputation as the company chaplain but will gain you little respect as a manager. You may also grow to hate all those people who talk your ear off. Being a lousy listener is a nice way of turning people off with little risk. There's nothing I've suggested here that your associates, spouses, children, and friends don't do to you regularly.

That's Your Problem

Now, the harshest exercise of all. It's like running a four-minute mile, because it involves the most social risk for you. People generally will be offended unless they know what you are doing. This exercise should be carefully planned and executed, probably first with those who love you. Here is how you do it, and why.

The way you do it is to accept responsibility for no one else's feelings. If someone says marketing feels you don't care about meeting production schedules, you say, "That's your problem. I do it as much as necessary." If your wife says, "The kids feel you don't pay any attention to them in the evenings," you say, "That's their problem. I'm tired."

For whatever reason, some people over the years take on the responsibility for everyone else's feelings and after awhile everyone leans on them. Their loved ones, their enemies, all tell them that the things they do make them sad, unhappy, hurt, and so on. They accept the responsibility even when they really don't think they should. The guilt piles up without rational cause, paralyzing them. Their willingness to accept it makes them a dumping ground for everyone's personal refuse. They forget about themselves, or run themselves into the ground. Think what they could achieve by unleashing all that energy tied up in feeling guilty!

I'm not so radical as to suggest that we don't all have some liability for each other's feelings, if only to try to ameliorate and soothe where possible. But if you find yourself feeling bad for everyone, you have probably built a pattern that encourages people to induce guilt into you.

Of course, you can say "That's your problem" in a milder way, such as, "You don't say," "My word," "Sorry you feel that way," or "I can see how you feel." They all add up to the same thing: trying to sort out when you should feel guilty and when it isn't your problem.

In this chapter we touched on a few of the things that make you discontented with your organizational lot. You are seen as Mr. Nice Guy, with all that that entails, and pushed further into that role by all those cocky, self-assured, successful bosses. It just looks like they don't want you to share in what they have.

You don't have to be content with that. This whole book is telling you that you can be more, or other, than what you are now as a middle manager. The "how to" for this change involves a lot of personal growth, and, as there are exercises for developing muscles, so are there exercises for developing people. Many trainers and behavioral scientists are hanging around your company door, right now, waiting to sell them to you or teach them to you, or apply them to you, or whatever. You must look at what you are, what they want to make you into, and what you really want to be.

On your own, however, you can stretch and begin to develop some new patterns of behavior. I gave you five exercises. They are concerned with your self-confidence, self-expression, identification of needs, preservation of time, and refusal to be responsible for other people's feelings. In the extreme, these exercises can turn you into a cocksure, verbally aggressive, demanding, rude, and callous person. Ideally, you will incorporate these concepts in some fashion with the nice guy you already are.

What are the risks for you? You could make a lot of people very angry, especially when you violate all those expectations of you they've built up over the years. You could, in the extreme, exercise yourself right out of a job or a marriage, but that is unlikely unless you are a fool. You are most likely to discover, much to your surprise, that people will respect you more, think more of your judgment, and be less likely to push you around. The long-term payoff is that you will not be such a Mr. Nice Guy at 45 that they have to carry you out on a stretcher. You will still be a vital human being with a lot to contribute.

12 | A Road Map for Self-Development

IN THIS CHAPTER I want to suggest a growth model for the middle manager to follow. While earlier chapters are of practical day-to-day use, this chapter is more of a personal, professional developmental framework. It sums up the need of everyone, especially middle managers, to think of himself as still in the process of developing, growing, and changing as a human being.

All of us can modify, on a self-help basis, some of our responses to life. We can examine our basic patterns with the help of an intimate friend and consciously pursue growth. Most of us are open to dramatic changes such as accompany religious conversion, change of vocation in middle life, or change of spouse and a different way of living with different friends. A few of us can even change some basic personality structure with intensive help of psychotherapy. Your success at pursuing your personal development will depend on your malleability, not on strength or weakness of character.

Your personal development is important to the company as well as to the rest of your life. Sometimes it is hard to sell the boss on a course workshop or laboratory dealing with the kinds of concerns outlined in this chapter. Management tends to measure results in the bottom right-hand corner, often in a cause-and-effect relationship. The clear connection between personal growth and the bottom right-hand corner is difficult to demonstrate.

148

Strictly from the point of view of the middle manager, I am sure that growing along the four suggested dimensions will permit the middle manager to go beyond the expected and get away with it more often. They are:

Becoming open to new ideas

Living fully in the present

Becoming genuine with others as well as with yourself

Becoming experimental

The balance of this chapter is a discussion of the risk-benefit ratio related to pursuing each developmental goal. Also included are "before-and-after" behavior patterns associated with each concern. Their polarities should be examined for their value, but with tongue in cheek. We are all a little bit "before" and a little bit "after" all the time.

BECOMING OPEN TO NEW IDEAS

Being open implies being free to examine and respond to the many facets of each situation without being limited by preset reactions: "We never do this. We never do that." In other words, it is a way of taking each situation encountered, each new piece of information received, or each new event participated in, and letting it tell its own story. This means being relatively free to suspend your prejudgments, stereotypes, and the narrowly conceived views of your associates, your company, your family, and your own potential.

Table 2 gives some before-and-after descriptions of the characteristics observed in people in relation to being open to new ideas. One column is before growth. The other represents a kind of apex of growth.

Being open is risky, too, not just virtuous. The risks seem clear, for when you are open you risk the possibility of being indecisive because of apparently being without judgment, with the ability to compare but with no condemnation or evaluative qualities. You may seem to be a nondecision maker because you are always open to new information. You may, if dogmatically seeking to become open, actually become a contemplator, an appreciator, and a noninterferer, with the philosophy of letting your employees go their own way, sometimes irresponsibly. In

Table 2.   *Orientation toward new ideas.*

BEFORE	AFTER
Perceives world as stable and change as an illusion. The world functions along specific, unchanging principles and verities.	Understands the world as "becoming," changing; recognizes stability as an illusion.
Applies general rules or practices with little regard for changes in circumstances.	Places stress on each circumstance and situation dictating its own ground rules.
Thinking is oriented to maintaining the status quo—don't rock the boat.	Is oriented toward change and new approaches.
Needs to know answers; looks for pat answers and facts. Controls boundaries of life to avoid uncertainties.	Tolerates uncertainties and ambiguities; sees only probabilities.
Does not question the structures within which he functions.	Has a constructive discontent with limitations of present structures.
Forces things to be logical, sequential, and identifiable so as to avoid following experiences and hunches that may defy logic.	Trusts intuition.
Overvalues and overdepends on the expert and on labels and roles in life.	Is open to the gifts and contributions of people regardless of their profession or professed expertise.
Depends on external authorities such as families, churches, or tradition to dictate values and proper rules for living.	Has an internal set of values, philosophy of life, or religion by which to live.

other words, you may simply accept anything and everything with great and undiscriminating tolerance, an intolerable state for a manager. In fact, such a manager is the stereotype of the old human-relations-oriented manager.

Then, why would you risk change in yourself toward greater openness? The answer is clear in the message of key behavioral scientists. If you can function more as an open person, you will find that:

—You can be free to think along new dimensions, to be innovative.

—You will find yourself more capable of responding spontaneously and appropriately to circumstances and events as they occur.

—Old stereotyped bases for decision making will be altered.

—Your thinking and decisions will be based on more creative, pragmatic approaches to each situation, broadening the creative scope of your mind.

—You will be less dependent on others' perceptions and more autonomous, more in charge of your life.

Openness to new ideas does not mean never making a decision, being fuzzy-headed, or having no position.

The middle manager who is open can be flexible, however, and not get caught in semantics with the boss or specific ideologies he wants to protect. As we noted earlier, the colonel in *The Bridge on the River Kwai* had developed tunnel vision. His world was so fixed that he couldn't allow new data to alter his present view of reality. Today the middle manager is besieged with new ideas: "Maybe it's O.K. to smoke grass (?)" "Maybe women should get as much money as men for comparable positions (?)" "Is God really dead (?)" "Can a president really be a crook (?)" "Is it really O.K. to get a divorce (?)" On and on the new challenges deliver their blows to what we thought were verities, if not ultimate, at least something to hold on to.

When, then, does one say as Martin Luther said, "Here I stand. I cannot do otherwise"? I suppose one should do this when one is ready to quit work permanently. For living itself is being in the nexus of what we think is a must and what we are actively discovering is not necessary after all. For that reason, being open is far less risky than being closed, most of the time.

LIVING FULLY IN THE PRESENT

The only time you really have is right now. Now is a summary of the past and pregnant with the future. So many of us live in such a way that life slips by without having been fully experienced. Live fully in the present, then, and use the past and the future by not wishing, wanting, or hoping for something in the present which you could have made possible but did not; not being tied by regret and guilt feelings to the past; not being immobilized "now" by what you hope might happen in the future.

In the balance of things, what you are doing now must be what you choose to do, or you wouldn't be doing it. If you really wished you were more aggressive, more involved, more loving, and so on, you would do it. Perhaps you say that you do not act this or that way because you are shy, or afraid. If so, you are simply saying that you *want more* to protect yourself in your shyness or your fear than you want to be aggressive, involved, or loving.

Being fully present in the now can be defined as a kind of state of being involving knowing how your body feels, knowing what your feelings are, being aware of the reactions of others around you, and concentrating fully on what *is*, right now. See Table 3 for some before-and-after characteristics.

Just as with openness, living fully in the present has its risks. It involves:

— Really letting go, throwing yourself into something.
— Fear that you may lose your objectivity, becoming overwhelmed through being involved; even losing your cool.
— Having to face up to what you are actually feeling in the deepest sense, even if you don't act on it.
— Recognizing that what you really want *is* what you are thinking, feeling, acting.
— Losing the habit of clock watching because you are immersed in people and events and what you want to make happen.
— Having to trust the future to grow out of being true to the present.

Why risk it? The possible gains of full awareness and participation are considerable. As you immerse yourself in the moment,

— Your feet are on the ground because you are grounded in what is most probably so, what can be ascertained; not what might have been or what may be — iffy kinds of thoughts and feelings.
— Because you are concentrating on right now, more of you is available to be effective.

Table 3. *Orientation toward living in the present.*

BEFORE	AFTER
Closes self off from feelings; not fully aware of own reactions.	Aware of personal feelings in the present moment.
Unable to respond fully with capacities for sensing; does not fully see or hear what is going on.	Able to use full capacities of the senses.
Not fully involved in the present moment; held back by past experiences, biases, and fears, or holding out for fulfillment of hopes for the future.	Assumes full participation in the present moment—the here and now; whole-hearted participation.
Avoids full awareness or exposure because of unwillingness to live with self.	Faces up to and lives with what he feels and knows self to be.
There are times to play and times to work.	Considers work and play inseparable.
Clock is a road map that everyone is expected to adhere to; not in touch with "real" feelings about what he wants; depends on clock to tell him when to eat, sleep, and so on.	Clock is only useful for designating times for mutual happenings; operates on wants and feelings; the clock does not determine his day.
Often perceives self as an observer or uninvolved.	Is a part of events around him.
Does not trust own feelings or capacities; fears he may not be up to coping with the unknown. Tends to overplan.	Trusts own abilities, feelings, and capacities to deal with the moment without excessive preparation.
Carries guilt, anger, and shame not appropriate to his present actions.	Feels guilt or anger appropriate to the circumstances.

—As a result of immersion in your senses and surroundings, you will be wiser.

—You will have a greater capacity for deep personal relationships, at almost momentary meeting.

—You will be more effective as an instrument of change in your business, in your community, and in your other associations; therefore you will be more powerful.

— You will sense great pleasure, ecstasy, and pain as you gain increased awareness of the world around you.
— You will reduce your frustration, which is often a product of unrealistic expectations.

Another approach to living fully in the present is to discuss briefly the concept of time management. Today there is greater interest than ever in time management because it seems "no one has the time." Courses are designed to teach managers how to establish priorities and choose among them. Books are sold on time management and everyone emphasizes quantity. However, I've yet to see any substantial discussion of the concept of quality; in other words, time competence.

Time competence means using the time you have competently, that is, fully. How many meetings do you sit through in which you have neither input nor interest? How long will you sit waiting in the boss's outer office? How many lengthy conversations with long-winded employees do you have? How many hours do you spend in front of the one-eyed monster looking at whatever happens to appear next? Are you really with people or are you preoccupied? The questions could continue, but I'm sure you see the trend. All of us have a time management problem. Living fully in the present means that a smaller proportion of our time is poorly used.

BECOMING GENUINE WITH OTHERS

This concept is based on the assumption that genuine self-expression is a sound basis for relating to others. It means being genuinely revealing of what you feel, think, act, and say with and toward other people. This may require you to be close and challenging to people, sharing your feelings and concerns with them, investing yourself in other people both positively and negatively. It requires the willingness to be what you are in the face of what you fear may be the reaction of other people. It means having less fear of criticism from others, less need to be liked by others, less fear of rejection. It means expecting your genuine self to be the most desirable gift you could give to others. Table 4 gives some descriptions of the before-and-after ways people operate in being genuine with others.

Becoming genuine has its dangers. For in honestly expressing

Table 4.   *Orientation toward being genuine with others.*

BEFORE	AFTER
Fails to reveal true feelings and self through actions with others.	Generally acts in harmony with his feelings.
Is controlled and stylized in relating to others.	Is spontaneous in actions and relationships.
Tries to put self across as a certain kind of person: nice, sharp, dignified, tough, tender.	Is willing to be perceived by others on the basis of his natural behavior.
Fails to communicate feelings or communicates only those he thinks he should have.	Communicates his feelings to the people involved.
Acts on the basis of what he thinks others expect.	Is free from overconcern for what other people think.
Is concerned about losing one's dignity or losing face, therefore, unwilling to risk rejection; works to assure self against rejection.	Is not overly fearful of appearing in a bad light, willing to risk rejection from others; thus is free from having to defend self.
Depends on the fulfillment of his needs through the response of others.	Makes fewer demands on others.
Holds back; avoids intimacy in personal relationships.	Is able to enter into intimate relationships.
Controls real feelings and wishes to avoid conflict.	Is willing to risk encounter with others through expression, what is felt, or experienced.
Is not free to risk the possibility of personal change.	Is willing to risk alteration of self through involvement with others.

what you are, you run the risk of exposing yourself to other people and being rejected. They may not like what they see; they may not handle you gently; or they may not be able to accept you for what you are. They may be frightened of you! They may not love you. Why risk it? Because through taking this kind of risk you may become:

— Freer from the strain and energy-sapping behavior of having to cover up, pretending to be somebody you really are not.
— More confident, abler to like and accept yourself.
— Better liked or accepted by some other people without the necessity of a personal facade with them.

- Abler to enter into meaningful, deeper relationships with others.
- Abler to straighten out tangles in understanding and working with others.
- Aware that it doesn't matter all that much when some people don't particularly like you.
- Somewhat relieved of physical complaints that have emotional causes or components.

Probably the greatest benefit in being genuine is that it means less compartmentalization in one's life. In other words, genuineness is a function of not having to be a hypocrite. When, as a manager, you are indignant to find that an employee has been pilfering the expense account, you'll want to be genuine in your response. Be as angry as you feel. If you've done the same at some time in the past, at least own up to yourself and be sympathetic. If you haven't done it yourself, then raise hell, but also remember, "Let the one without sin cast the first stone." Genuineness also means nonhypocrisy—having your feet in the clay with the rest of us.

I think of people whose business behavior is so different from that in the home, in the hunting lodge, or in Las Vegas. Such fragmentation leads to a lack of consistent self-image and helps develop the game-playing routine. I've often administered the FIRO-B questionnaire [1] to businessmen. It purports to measure interpersonal needs. During the analysis some people often say, "I wasn't sure whether to think of my home or my office when answering the questions. Does that have an effect on the test?" The question itself makes an assumption that one can legitimately *be* different. There is no way in my mind that a person who is genuine can have that kind of severe dichotomy in values and behavior. I hate to give this answer, but it's a fact: "Your ungenuineness is showing!"

A couple of years ago a magazine ran an article about a young executive who went home at night, took off his square suit, put on his kimono, smoked grass, and lived a nonexecutive, off-hour life. Our corporations often reward middle managers for being one way in the company and another at the PTA. Both cases are unhealthy situations.

Being genuine, then, means having a continuity in your values and behavior so that anywhere I find you, under any conditions, I won't have to say, "Is that Mary? Is that really George?"

BECOMING EXPERIMENTAL

This concern clearly relates to the middle manager's creativity, but also to his willingness to move mountains. In general, companies are not experimental. The more production oriented they are, the less they are interested in new ideas—no matter how many suggestion boxes they have to impress the unions. To be an experimental manager means having a willingness to try new approaches, such as appear in the next unit of this book. But before we get into that, let's examine Table 5 for some before-and-after behavioral patterns.

Table 5. *Orientation toward being experimental.*

BEFORE	AFTER
Simply seeks to cope with the problems his behavior sometimes causes others.	Sets short-term goals and works actively to achieve them.
Usually feels there is a right and a wrong way.	Tends to find it hard to settle on one alternative. Sees values of each.
Is fearful of attempting an untried method or idea.	Is willing to let a new thing or idea prove itself.
Wants to be assured of success before attempting a project or making a decision.	Is willing to propose and try alternatives with awareness that trials may fail.
Uses failure or mistakes as a reason for avoiding risk in the future.	Uses a failure or mistake as a learning experience; puts it to constructive use.
Always desires a rational approach to problem solving.	Uses fantasy and "what if" methods as a legitimate way to explore alternatives (for example, synectics).
Tends to consider risk as a top priority when considering alternatives.	When exploring alternatives doesn't consider risk as the most important consideration.
Considers self as uncreative.	Sees self as creative.
Fears the worst possible consequences from the future.	Has faith in the overall goodness of the consequences of the future.

You can systematically pursue alternatives of choice and action and, by exploring them, greatly improve your chances of finding viable alternatives to your present behavior in both your personal and business lives. In other words, becoming experimental involves reaching out and trying to find new ways of working with concepts, actions, and feelings and attempting to put them into use — making them work for you and your organization.

When you attempt new ways of thinking and behaving toward others, you are taking the chance that it's not going to work out. You risk

- Bumbling, error, and out-and-out failure.
- The possibility of overextending yourself, getting hurt, failing in your own eyes and in the eyes of others.
- Entertaining new ideas that shake up that which you used to take for granted.
- Having to admit that you have been responsible for making an error in judgment.
- Fear that you will not make a sound decision. You waver too long and an opportunity is lost; or you plunge right in without enough careful thought — and blunder unnecessarily.
- Fear that change will not be easily created, resulting in an attempt to deal with each situation of change in the same way, with the same methods.

A major inhibition to being personally experimental is the fear of failure. This fear may be expressed through overconfidence and consequent overextending, or you may be underconfident and fail to assert yourself and to achieve appropriate expectations of yourself. Fear of failure may affect your relationships with authorities and experts in several ways:

- You may attempt to ridicule or backbite in order to demonstrate your superiority.
- You may resent others for having more information and authority than you do.
- You may become excessively dependent on what others say and fail to use your own initiative when you should.

Fear is a funny thing: If you are a little afraid, you tend to do better than you might otherwise do. If you are too afraid, you will hold back or fail to act. Experience has shown that the best way to beat fear is to gradually learn to cope with the kinds of experiences of which you are afraid until repeated experience has wiped out your fear altogether. You will always have fear of failure to some degree when venturing into new possibilities. Creative risk taking shows a way to cope with this fear. Have the courage to fail if necessary. Learn by your failure. Try again; find a new route. Know that no failure is ever final, only momentary.

As you consider and pursue each alternative you will probably find some people who will support you in your thinking and efforts and others who will oppose you. Why risk it? Because becoming experimental is imperative to your functioning as an autonomous person, that is, being one who creates and guides the forces of change in the world around you. Then, too, as Allport said, "While we learn dependable modes of reducing tension, we also abandon old habits and take risks in searching out new courses of conduct. It is only through risk and variation that growth can occur." [2]

In this chapter we suggested a road map for self-development. The pathways we discussed as being primary were being open to new ideas; living fully in the present; being genuine with others as well as oneself; and being experimental. The idealized behavior that these four attributes represent is characteristic only of those persons who are fully realizing their potential and are fully developed. But, of course, who has ever met one? The message of the chapter is that the path of development, while long, is worth careful planning and pursuit by the middle manager.

UNIT FOUR
ORGANIZATIONAL RISK MANAGEMENT

GOOD MANAGEMENT is always correlated with management of risk. Insurance protects against loss, and few companies today would be without it. Companies also sign agreements with professional employees to protect the company with "no compete" clauses. Decisions that incur increased costs for the expectation of some greater return are always carefully made. Regardless of whether the word "risk" is ever used, it is clear that risk taking is a preoccupation of management. Chapter 13 outlines some of the factors to consider in determining if management is controlling the risks that are detrimental to effective management.

In Chapter 14 we suggest a way by which you can examine whether you have the right people to begin the strategy of risk reduction called organizational development (OD). A way to start an OD program is described in some detail in Chapter 15, followed by a method to deal with potential interorganizational headaches. Chapter 16 offers strategies of negotiation among the various groups in a company.

13 | Checklist of Organizational Risk Factors

THE MIDDLE MANAGER has a tendency to focus on what's on his plate. The result for the corporation is that decisions made often do not properly take into account the broader picture of the company's areas of potential risk. Any risk management program is based on being sensitive and responsive to these areas. Any good manager's job is to control risk. This chapter reviews the business and management environment for the areas of continuous risk in which the company operates. Naturally, the reader is aware of all of these factors, but here you will have a chance to reflect on them and do a self- or company assessment. If you say, "This doesn't apply to me," you may be limiting your advancement in the company. The manager who does not reflect full knowledge of these factors rarely commands the respect of his associates in the decision-making process.

The risk factors examined here are risks of a different order than those dealing with the protection of inventories, or against calamities, or involved in buying a new plant location. The organizational risk factors in this discussion focus on two areas: environmental factors and internal organizational factors.

THE ENVIRONMENT

First, let's consider the environment in which the company does business. The environment represents the market for the company, and the resources the company needs to be productive; it also establishes the conditions under which that company must operate. Therefore, no matter what the product, no matter how competitive, and no matter how excellent and open the management is, all is for naught in a hostile environment. The corporation, then, must attempt to control the risk in its environment.

Either intuitively or systematically, managers scan the company's environment constantly looking for potential areas of exposure to new or historical risk. A current policy or practice of the company may be encouraging excessive risks that must be reduced. For example, a toy manufacturer may discover that a stuffed toy is flammable. While the company may get by with producing and selling the toy, the risks to the company are excessive. If a child dies, the public is indignant, regulatory agencies inspect every product of the company, new, more restrictive legislation is passed, the board of directors fires the president, and the company's customers lose confidence in all of its products. I've painted the worst possible picture, but it could and has happened in just that way. Unless managers are constantly alert to risks they are taking, they may well find themselves in a hostile environment.

Political Factors

The company must insure that its political environment is relatively stable. The tactic here is to reduce risk, not to take any new ones. The company doesn't want the notoriety received by IT&T in 1972. Such notoriety invites new, controlling legislation. The company's lobbyists will seek good relations with governments. Such relationships might, at some point, help get a restriction removed, an easement abandoned, a special exemption made to bypass an interstate commerce regulation. Unless carefully watched, the company may suffer from discriminatory legislation, market or price controls, or political badgering at the hand of a legislator looking for publicity. Constant surveillance means being able to reduce the risk of an unpredictable political climate.

Regulatory Agencies

Regulatory agencies can put a company out of business overnight. Such incidents as cyclamates in soft drinks, mercury in canned fish, abrasives in cosmetics, flammable children's clothing—all can be dealt with in a variety of ways. The agency can simply warn the company, take the company to court, get a court order for immediate recall of the product, do it quietly, splash it in the papers, interpret the regulation leniently or harshly. Therefore the kind of relationship with such agencies is the key to company success: Good relationships reduce risk; bad ones increase the harshness of rulings.

The Public

Today, more than ever, companies must carefully cultivate their public image. Mass media make even the vilest, wildest rumor credible. The taconite industry struggles with the public over asbestos particles in the drinking water of Duluth, Minnesota. The industry says the quantity of particles isn't damaging. The public says any is too much.

Nader's Raiders and other public interest groups, such as the Minnesota Public Interest Research Group, push not only the corporation but even government agencies into action. Thus Ralph Nader demands a safety commission be appointed by the secretary for transportation. MPIRG demands that the FDA be stricter in applying regulations on common hazards of toilet articles. These and other demands are signs of growing public interest groups, better organized and financed, that will act as constraints on company freedoms.

The Board of Directors and Stockholders

Normally, stockholders have a single-mindedness about their investments: they want a healthy return. Boards of directors have the primary responsibility to see that stockholders' investments are protected and fair gains realized. Therefore, they act as a constraining force on spending money. Generally, they are not prone to seeking windfall profits; rather, they are more satisfied with annual incremental gains with low to moderate risks. Management must take the board into account because it can hire and fire top and sometimes middle management. Boards have little tolerance for long-term profit slides. This may be why the terms of corporation presidents seem shorter and shorter. A president usually has one year to turn a long-term profit slide around.

Market Needs

One of the constraints a company has is simply whether the world needs or wants the service or product it provides. If such is not the case, the company has three alternatives: it can go out of business, switch products, or risk advertising to create a market. Advertising may pay off and reduce market risk, or it may lead to myriad problems. Advertising firms can ruin a company through overkill. Too many excessive claims for a new product may bring regulatory agencies down on corporate heads. In the end, even advertising can't sell freezers to an Eskimo. The fact is, advertising is a dynamic risk, perhaps one you can't afford not to take, with heavy potential loss or gain. You must constantly be aware of the odds.

Competitive Companies

Another major uncontrollable factor is the competition, especially if it is aggressive. The competition hits the marketplace with the idea of taking all or part of the business. It will lose money to get a toehold. Information on the marketing, production, and engineering decisions of competitors is the major element by which to reduce this risk. The best source of such information is your customer, and that is one reason why good informal client relationships reduce risk.

Client Relationships

As we have just pointed out, client relationships are essential to understanding what the competition is doing. They are a further resource because they are constantly telling you—openly or guardedly, knowingly or unknowingly—what new products they need. They may also give you information on the needs of similar organizations not yet your customers. The better the formal and informal relations with clients, the less risk the company has from loss to the competition.

Suppliers

Suppliers are sometimes the lifeblood of a company. A consulting firm must have good subcontractors working for it. A car manufacturer needs a good relationship with steel manufacturers. Newspapers need paper. Most every industry has suppliers and must maintain good relationships with them in order to be first on the preferred list to receive reserves in case of a strike, or to have materials delivered on time, even if everyone else must wait. To reduce risk, good relationships must be maintained and, where possible, backup suppliers identified or created.

Employee Families

In such a list of factors, the average person in business may well wonder how employee families can be considered as company resources. They may not be on the payroll but they work for or against the company all the time. Their attitude toward the company is crucial. A hostile spouse can keep a valuable employee from joining the firm or cause one to leave. A hostile family can make a simple location change a nightmare. Disgruntled employee families can certainly influence community opinions of the company. Positive relationships with families can result in greater freedom for employees, stronger morale among employees, and better informal relationships with the public in general.

Lending Institutions

Lending institutions must be hospitable for companies to survive. The source of capital must never dry up or the company will not be able to meet the crises that all companies face from time to time. Then, too, any expansion always takes capital and new money must be available.

Along with stockholders, the lending institution, itself bound by regulatory agencies, is the prime money source. For small companies, personal relationships with bankers, enabling them to operate with initimate knowledge of their affairs, are the greatest assets. Large corporations use such assets as real estate, inventories, or personal guarantees of directors for collateral. Misusing lending officers is like misusing your heart. It is a high risk venture.

Protective Associations

Then, too, there are protective associations the company must join, too numerous to mention, except for a few examples: the chamber of commerce, the National Association of Manufacturers, the American Institute of Architects. These associations are constantly lobbying to prevent discriminatory legislation or rulings against their particular industry. They also seek favorable rulings for their members with all levels of government. In a society where large numbers of people banded together can influence government better than the single company or person, no company can afford to go it alone. Associations are watchdogs against incursion on the property and privileges of the company.

Manpower Pool

Today's corporations are highly dependent on the sophisticated technical and managerial talent produced by the educational institutions of our society. Many corporations, sensitive to this fact, and to the huge expense of education, often reduce the risk of not getting adequate manpower in the future by giving money or providing help in various forms to academic or training schools.

Some companies, for instance, offer four-year scholarships and, upon graduation of the recipient, contact him or her concerning future employment. States offer their professional employees continuing education programs through which they can further their education at state expense by contracting to work a certain number of years for the state. ROTC finances college students to further its own ends. All branches of the armed forces and the U.S. Public Health Service will pick up part of the tab for doctors and other professionals in return for a work commitment. Some wealthy businessmen are willing to invest in the future by endowing training schools. Unions provide apprenticeship programs to control and insure the supply of skilled workmen.

Manpower pump-priming is a necessity if corporations don't want their pool of human resources to dry up.

As an exercise toward determining the current effectiveness of your risk reduction in the environment, answer the questions in the checklist on environment. The majority of your answers should be in the yes column if your company is indeed in touch with and controlling the risk factors in its environment. If the answers are primarily no, then you and your company should be

CHECK YOUR ENVIRONMENT

	Yes	No	Unknown
Is your company sensitive to and in touch with political bodies?	___	___	___
Are regulatory agencies cooperative?	___	___	___
Is the company's public image good?	___	___	___
Are directors supportive of new ventures?	___	___	___
Are market needs known, and is your company creating them where necessary?	___	___	___
Do you know what the competition is doing?	___	___	___
Do middle managers feel responsible for reducing environmental risks?	___	___	___
Do suppliers see you as a preferred customer?	___	___	___
Are customer relationships, both formal and informal, tops?	___	___	___
Do employee families talk up the company?	___	___	___
Have lending institutions developed a willingness to risk money on your company?	___	___	___
Does the company actually support protective associations?	___	___	___
Has the company made adequate provisions to protect its sources of manpower?	___	___	___

working together, with outside help if necessary, to develop appropriate steps to reduce current risk levels.

If your answers are mostly unknown, then your view is too narrow and you may have tunnel vision, a disability often associated with middle management. In that case there are some specific actions you can take to broaden your perspective. These include volunteering and taking more responsibility (see Chapter 10), pushing for more information through organizational development approaches (see Chapter 15), or taking other personal ways suggested in later chapters in this book.

INTERNAL ORGANIZATIONAL PROCESSES

The second major risk area to be evaluated is that of the effectiveness of the company's internal processes. While environmental factors are volatile and unpredictable because they are relatively immune to direct manipulation, the internal processes of the company are like one's family. Direct influence can be exerted through rewards, requests, orders, and the like.

Of course, whether people comply is another matter. There are many ways employees circumvent management's wishes without seeming to be insubordinate. David Brown gives some of the commoner forms of noncompliance:

> The worker can revise the quality of what is asked.
> He can revise the quantity.
> He can revise the time schedule.
> He can revise the priority.
> He can revise the procedures he has been told to use.
> He can try to convince the boss that the job doesn't need to be done.
> He can claim he doesn't have the proper equipment (or manpower or ability).
> He can claim that he is too busy.
> He can claim that it is contrary to existing policy, that it won't work, or that someone else should do it.
> He can make a scene or threaten to appeal to higher authority.
> He can become ill and remain at home.
> He can do nothing at all.
> He can do something else and say that this covers what was wanted.
> He can give lip service but show others how they can "get around it."
> He can assign (redelegate) the job to someone else.
> He can *over*-comply, or he can do a variety of other things that cancel the effect of what was wanted.[1]

Some of the major variables needing constant examination for relative risk levels are planning, control systems, communication, and organization. Under each of these, a variety of questions must be answered to determine the present levels of corporate risk taking. These are the processes that convert the environmental input into the final product. Without effective planning, controlling, communicating, and organizing, the company will not be able to convert its resources, take advantage of its environment, and produce at a respectable return on its investment. How these factors are handled increases or decreases the company's risk position.

Planning

Planning still tends to be a dirty word in many industries. Even financial planning is relatively new and has developed only as new accrual accounting systems and rapid computers have made it increasingly accurate and useful to management. Unfortunately, neither marketing plans nor manpower plans has the serious attention of most management.[2]

Ideally, planning should be the activity by which an organization becomes and remains integrated and single-minded in its efforts, thus lowering the risk of a shotgun approach which never hits a target. In some companies the owner plans on the back of an envelope while sitting under a palm tree. In other cases planning is a practical activity developed by senior management with a great deal of input from the various departments. In still other cases planning is a highly complex attempt at integrating grass roots needs, expert knowledge, budget, manpower concerns, and political considerations.[3] The middle manager with savvy and a little luck can urge planning on his top management if it has not taken planning seriously. If top management isn't interested, the middle manager can still do it in his own department in a limited way.

In thinking about planning, you must consider those functions that reduce business risk, especially risks in the environment. These include the following:

Identify and define the corporate or department mission. It is very important that the organization (or department) know what business it is in. Companies that founder are often lost on the shoals of disparate missions. Resources are spread too thin. Decisions are made purely opportunistically. Medium-size companies that do well are often "better mousetrap" companies. They have a single product line, a good set of customers, and simply have a high quality and single-mindedness.

Define the marketplace and objectives for a given period of time. In order to fulfill the mission the company will have to project its financial goals, product or service development goals, and manpower needs. These needs should be built around serving a defined market.

Gather and maintain a factual and statistical information base. This goes without saying, but in some companies it isn't done well or systematically. Current updating on finances, market, and trends in one's industry is indispensable to good planning.

Make projection of future-anticipated variables important to the company's decision making. Acquisitions, mergers, going public, and so on.

Lay out alternative courses of action with relative costs and benefits to the company. Too often in the medium- or small-size company one way jumps out and everyone gets on the bandwagon. But good planning means really letting various strategies develop, and then choosing the one or ones that fit your pocketbook and expectations for return on investment.

Install a systematic feedback system to evaluate company performance. Use those computers for something besides bookkeeping. This function will keep you in touch with the backend of planning, where it usually fails. Make sure your company goals, department goals, and goals for smaller units are stated in terms of measurable outputs. The general tendency is to use statements of intent and input rather than expected results.

There are some fundamentals of planning processes that seem to bring about the most real and effective planning, especially if it is for more than a year. These include

Make sure all units of the organization participate in the planning. Include input from all levels of employees. They don't necessarily want to vote but they would like to know that they matter to the company's future.[4]

Coordinate objectives and plans from all units. If a mechanism for joint influencing and informing of objectives isn't provided for, the accomplishment of one unit's plans may unintentionally put another unit out of business. In one demonstration school the research organization's goals included the cooperation of all academic departments. The only problem was that the other departments had never seen the research department's goals. Therefore, they might well not cooperate even without knowing it, thus undermining the research department.

Insure that line managers rather than staff bear responsibility for planning. Only the manager, ultimately accountable, can make real plans. Staff personnel help by gathering the data and, maybe, by creating alternatives and procedures. But the manager who lets staff people do the work will never have the sense of propriety for the objectives needed for their accomplishment.

Time planning cycles to coincide with business cycles. Smaller organizations within large corporations should also time their planning to the corporation's business planning cycle.

Communicate objectives and plans to the entire organization. Books of objectives are worthless unless specific review means are set up by which people understand and appreciate the objectives of those parts of the organization that interface with theirs.

Insure that evaluation data are fed into the decision-making process and that appropriate revisions are timely. Nothing is riskier than a plan that is inappropriate. In some ways no plan at all is less risky. At least no one is fooling himself that a plan really exists.

Now, check your planning (page 174).

Control System

In large organizations, control systems are needed to predict how and for what purpose human and material resources will be used. Sometimes control systems are misused by managers who utilize employee information simply to control them. This practice is so common that employees are generally suspicious of any control systems. People fear regimentation, increased dependence, exploitation by management—in general, being made to feel organizationally impotent.

Ideally, control systems provide a two-way street for management and employees to influence each other in decision making and the achievement of goals. Through company objective setting, employees could tell their story to management and have an opportunity to sell an idea and to create their own jobs. Management, however, is usually preoccupied with objectives of its own which it wants to convince the employee to adopt. There are, of course, exceptions where joint goal setting between super-

CHECK YOUR PLANNING

	Yes	No	Unknown
Does the planning staff provide information management needs for making decisions?	___	___	___
Are the goals and objectives of the company stated in measurable output terms within a reasonable time frame?	___	___	___
Are decisions about the future based on full consideration of alternative choices?	___	___	___
Do line managers take responsibility for planning activities?	___	___	___
Are all employees aware of the company's long-range goals and the shorter range objectives?	___	___	___
Do employees of each unit participate in developing the objectives and strategies for their particular unit?	___	___	___
Is there general commitment among employees to achieve the company objectives?	___	___	___
Does the planning staff relate to top-level management?	___	___	___
Does the planning cycle of activities take place at logical times in the production and marketing cycle of the company?	___	___	___
Is evaluation of the company's products or performances fed back to managers in time to make necessary changes?	___	___	___
Is structure planning an activity that is valued by top managers?	___	___	___

visor and supervisee is actually done. In this atmosphere the risk of not accomplishing these objectives is considerably reduced.

Control systems also allow greater individual differences to exist. Bereft of explicit objectives for employees, managers often are quite nervous. They develop a nervous need to know exactly what "they" are doing. The more "they" are doing the same thing, the easier it is to tell who is doing poorly and who is doing well.

Through various and effective joint objective-setting processes each individual's goals can be known. I consider such a process more control than planning, although, of course, it is both. Each employee's objectives can be permitted to be quite different from a co-worker's because, under these conditions, performance will be measured by how well individual objectives are accomplished. Again, a good idea which releases the employee from demotivating conformity is ignored, almost totally. Management doesn't want to risk the certainty of direct control for the uncertainty of higher motivation and productivity.

Middle managers, taking their cues from top management and juggling top management needs and employee production, may actually obstruct employee satisfaction and effectiveness. Caught between top management and employee demands, middle managers meddle more than necessary, or useful, with day-to-day activities about which they may actually know little. When an objectives system is employed, they may well be tempted to use it simply to look good with top management, but really just continue business as usual. After all, there are few rewards in most businesses to prompt employees to tell management what they really are doing. It's like asking an adolescent to talk everything over with the family. The employee or adolescent may indeed do so, but only to avoid punitive action.

Check your company's control system for its usefulness and see how much risk of being controlled your employees have to take if they really want to cooperate (page 176).

Communication

Most management consultants talk about morale or attitudes; usually, they view these as feelings of people who can be manipulated like children by top management. They suggest that managers treat employees like one would small children. By implication, John is crying, but if he's handed a new toy his face lights up and he stops crying until something goes wrong again.

Such an approach seldom gets at the real problems that underlie the questions on an attitude questionnaire, by far the most accepted method today of trying to determine the needs of employees. As I understand Herzberg,[5] what he says regarding the

Check Your Control System

	Yes	No	Unknown
Are the bean counters excessively scrupulous and dominating?	____	____	____
Are clearances given in a reasonable time?	____	____	____
Do managers have responsibility for their own budgets?	____	____	____
Are report forms generally reasonable?	____	____	____
Is the objectives system for groups and individuals effective and accepted?	____	____	____
Are objectives of suborganization parts clear to employees?	____	____	____
Are controller requirements reasonable?	____	____	____
Is performance evaluation fair?	____	____	____
Are decisions made at lowest appropriate levels?	____	____	____
Do top and middle management get accurate information about problems?	____	____	____
Do policies assist rather than constrict?	____	____	____
Are there clear role expectations among employees?	____	____	____
Are middle managers overcontrolling supervisors?	____	____	____

insatiable quality of employee demands for happiness is that most attitude surveys will always show a level of dissatisfaction. These surveys usually are tuned in to hygienic demands of money, working conditions, supervisory attention, and fringe benefits. People never get enough of those.

Communication actually has to do more with the culture, the values, and the management style—be it authoritarian, benevolently authoritarian, consultative, or participative.[6] It looks at behavior related to decisions on how and whether people work together to get the job done. As they work together, what is the level of feeling they allow one another to express?

Communication, then, has a broader meaning than that associated with behaviorism. It means how people are treated by each other, whether discrimination is present, how effective meetings are in general, and whether there are too many or not enough. In other words, anything that has to do with how individuals and groups relate to one another, vertically and laterally, verbally and nonverbally. When you are assessing current risk levels in present management practice, answer the questions in the checklist on communication (page 178).

Organization

The risk involved in organizing is not simply the formal organization chart but the effectiveness and effective relationships between the formal and informal organization. Included u..der organizational risks are the more traditional concerns such as delegation practices and reorganization. Are top managers delegating authority along with responsibility? In Chapter 6 we suggested that perhaps they weren't. Are middle managers delegating to their subordinates? What about project managers? Are they given responsibility without budget control?

Organizations willing to risk the certainty of some loss of day-to-day control can bet that human initiative will cause greater productivity.[7] One spinoff from such a policy would be wider span of control, depending on the organization, its particular mission, and how much support and day-to-day supervision is needed. However, management's tendency is to overorganize and oversupervise, to narrow the span. Middle managers are already threatened by computerized supervision by which top management can know what is happening without the intervening variable called middle management. It may be that if employees really need less supervision, many middle manager jobs will no longer be important, depending again upon the industry, the organization's mission, and technology.

I'm certain that quite unconsciously top management wants a buffer between it and line supervisors. However, I've also seen top management consistently undercut true delegation. I think the

CHECK YOUR COMMUNICATION

	Yes	No	Unknown
Is there teamwork among management itself?	___	___	___
Are groups and committees effective in this company?	___	___	___
Is there excessive backbiting?	___	___	___
Is there discrimination by sex, age, race, and so on?	___	___	___
Overall, are people open or deceptive with one another?	___	___	___
Is there excessive competition between individuals or segments of the organization?			
Does middle management trust top management?	___	___	___
Is there a general climate of trust rather than mistrust?			
Is there excessive turf protection between managers?	___	___	___
Are managers generally accessible to employees?	___	___	___
Is there repetition of the same kind of troubles?	___	___	___
Is there a consistent loss of valuable employees?	___	___	___
Is there general disowning of responsibility for cause?	___	___	___
Is there too much slippage between decisions and action?	___	___	___
Are people adequately informed of or involved in new policies, program changes, and other information they need?			
Does the informal power structure have more power than the formal organizational structure?			

reason is simple. Unless top management is very busy dealing with the environment, it wants to run the company's daily operation. It is like the extra pair of hands behind Marcel Marceau: you see middle management's face, but the hands belong to top management. When middle management is really good, top management isn't necessary to daily operations. When the supervisors are really good, middle management isn't needed in specific projects. In whose self-interest does today's cumbersome, top-heavy organization work?

Finally, I suppose the best organizational structure is one that fits the job and the people. Reorganization should probably be as regular as any other management change based on both people's particular talents in the organization and what needs to get done. For organizations that lose 25 percent of their employees a year, certainly reorganization should, at a minimum, be done annually. Reorganization today tends to be used as *reagonization*: as times for reduction in force, or for demoting in such a fluid situation that no one can tell if what was done was fair or not. When more self-interest is being served than rational management taking place, the company is risking loss of good personnel and increased distrust of top management's objectives by its middle management.

Perhaps the way your organization now works is meeting individual self-interest, but does it really meet company interests? Check the chart on organization (page 180).

This chapter stresses the need for managers to be in touch with what psychologists call the force field. What are the forces in the company's environment that affect its survival and success? Two kinds of force fields exist and interrelate — those that impinge on and feed the corporation and those that convert those energies into a product or service.

We've examined a series of external factors that, when properly handled, reduce risk. These include federal, state, and local governments; regulatory agencies; the public; the board of directors; market needs; competitors; supplier and client relationships; employee families; lending institutions; protective associations; and the potential manpower pool.

Internal processes include how effectively the functions of planning are used and the extent to which personnel are involved.

CHECK YOUR ORGANIZATION

	Yes	No	Unknown
Is the organization top-heavy with managers?	___	___	___
Does top management use middle managers as puppets?	___	___	___
Does each management level avoid real delegation to the next?	___	___	___
Is there too great a difference between the organization chart and how things are really done?	___	___	___
Are secretaries peons?	___	___	___
Is the company overorganized?	___	___	___
Does the company regularly use reorganization as a way to get rid of people?	___	___	___
Is your organization too much like a military unit?	___	___	___
Has your company really tackled job redesign and enrichment?	___	___	___
Are organizational subparts too discrete?	___	___	___
Do organizational subparts have too many overlapping responsibilities?	___	___	___
Is your organization geared for work rather than for power needs of certain individuals?	___	___	___

Then, too, the methods by which controls are exercised directly affect morale, productivity, creativity, and the amount of self-starting behavior. Communication, the catchword for screwed up relationships, also needs careful examination for giving clues to the human climate within the organization. Finally, we examined factors related to the organization itself and how they can prevent as well as help productivity.

14 | Organizational Development
An Organizational Risk Reduction Strategy

LET'S ASSUME that you have assessed the risk factors in your environment and in your current organizational processes. Where do you go from there? The only place left is inside the people in the organization—a big, confusing step. In taking that step there are two primary areas of information you should master.

First, take a good, long look at the raw material in your organization—the people. Are they healthy, competent individuals? By healthy, I mean, are employees having blackouts? Is sick leave being used up? Are people being physically and psychologically burnt out or not being psychologically challenged? One can have too much or too little of anything. Health also includes the use of alcohol and drugs, and emotional as well as physical development. Competence covers what Floyd Mann, formerly of the Institute of Social Research at the University of Michigan, calls the necessary mix of management competencies: technical skills, organization skills, and human relations skills.

THE PEOPLE: CAN THEY DO THE JOB?

We are now at the crux of the matter. Can these people do the required job? Some people are wrong for your company. Some people mixed with other people are wrong. Some may be wonderful folks but still not have adequate technical skills. As a manager you must insure that they don't injure your team and your company. You must insist on high standards and self-discipline. Relocate those who fall behind. Not to do any of these things is risky. In fact, failure to do so breaks all three risk-taking rules: risking a lot for a little, not really considering the odds, and risking more than you can afford to lose.

Then, once you have assessed your group individually, you must have at your disposal the tool by which you can match the people to the environment, diagnose the risk level, and alter it if necessary. Throughout this entire process, you must remember what we discussed before, that the question is not whether change should take place but only the direction and areas in which that change should occur. What are your goals?

The following areas should be examined to determine if your people have the emotional and physical health and competence necessary to make that complex, objective process called an organization run at its peak performance.

Managerial Risks

In Chapter 8 we discussed at some length the various kinds of risk takers. In this context it becomes important, because no company wants excessive numbers of any one kind of risk taker. Organizations need a rational mixture of risk taking and creativity. They can't afford to have all repeaters or they will go out of business. They can't afford to have all innovators or they may never produce and market anything. In general, then, depending on the company's mission and requirements, it needs a mix of styles. Companies gain a reputation for being low or high risk, and attract people of similar ilk. Beware of being overloaded with green visors or daredevils.

Optimism Versus Cynicism

One serious problem plagues companies that hire too many people who are either Pollyannas or bad-mouthers. The Pollyannas can spend the company's money without appropriate planning. The cynics can destroy morale and undermine any positive efforts of management to improve the company. I've seen many management training programs undercut by an excessive amount of company critics who refer to it as "the company charm school." These cynics sit through presentations and always discuss the negative aspects. They always see management as the bad guys, as exploiters. But the greatest fault of the cynics is hypocrisy. They always hint at how a much better world could exist, but they never try to build it. While often individually helpful to the company, collectively cynics are destructive and a risky group.

Motivation Orientation

Atkinson[1] and McClelland[2] have focused much of their attention on the motivation called achievement. For business it may be the most important of all motivations. Motivation toward power leads toward the creation of greater bureaucracies. Motivation built on needs for affiliation leads toward less return on investment because of lower productivity. Achievement motivation, while in excess can lead toward excessive physical and mental stress, can also produce greater productivity and return on investment.[3] Business should create a climate of hard work that emphasizes and rewards achievement motivation, or else it risks being uncompetitive and less contributing to job satisfaction.[4]

Again, the ideal is a good balance. Where possible, a company should create a climate in which people with all three human motivations can receive satisfaction, not just the hot pilots and go-getters.[5] Other values than achieving are important to people, and must be satisfied or they will indeed become burnt out and lack self-development as fully functioning people.

Stimulants and Depressants

"A little wine is good for the stomach," said St. Paul, but the incidence of alcoholism in business detracts from getting the job done. It is estimated that nationally one out of fourteen persons are excessive drinkers at best and probably could be called alcoholics. The use of alcohol to decrease the stress, unleash more uninhibited behavior, and, in general, to alter the mind can have destructive effects on corporate life.

Companies sometimes do try to deal with the problem. One

company prohibits drinking at lunch. Others discourage alcohol at company parties. Firestone refuses to let men in the plant if they have missed appointments with their counselors. Some don't make rules at all. The point here is that if a company has too many heavy users of any stimulant or depressant, it isn't getting a full day's work from the troops. If the restrooms smell of marijuana or the boss's breath is foul at 10 A.M., the company is in trouble. Everyone recognizes the staggers in its various forms. How many companies are not dealing with the problem?[6]

Obsolete People

Many industries and businesses today face an increasing gap between the technical demands of their market and the ability of their employees to perform. All employees face a threat to their future employment because, unless they are in retraining programs—either on the job or in formal education institutions—they are fast becoming obsolete.

Although not a business, the United States Agency for International Development is currently going through a changeover that graphically illustrates what happens in a changing marketplace. For years the Agency provided technical assistance in agricultural technology, public administration, education, civil engineering, and other similar fields. Through US/AID Americans went to foreign countries and helped to build dams, roads, schools, and ministries, write books, create training, and do all the other necessary related tasks.

Then the nature of the Agency changed as the new thrust became institution building. The new concept was to help the country to help itself. Dollars followed dollars in grants and loans. Aid technicians wiped the dirt off their feet, washed their hands, and began to sit in the foreign ministries. Their new task was to work with and for the ministry as the American counterpart. The Americans helped the people develop their ideas, examine their own resources, and commit their own people to those goals.

Today, once again the strategy is changing. AID technicians are now brokers between foreign ministries and universities, private sectors, or nonprofit corporations in the United States that can provide technical assistance. AID technicians must work with unilateral agencies such as the World Bank, no longer dealing directly with a ministry. They recruit, but then get out of the way, being primarily managers, with requirements for technical competence in agriculture or education being secondary.

These changes can be replicated in a variety of organizations. The organization going through such transformation not only will face a crisis of perceived competence but will, in fact, have employees who lose self-esteem and become unable to operate in the new situation. Midcareer changes, retraining, self-renewal programs, and other manpower adjustments and planning, along with spending lots of dollars, are the only ways the company can avoid having an obsolete workforce.

People Who Can't Trust

Some people are mistrusters and haters. That language may seem strong from a behavioral scientist, but for organization purposes it must be said. They hold deep grudges and develop hate lists of corporate enemies. They should go or grow. Their existence in the company is destructive.

Emotions

Other people are out of touch with their feelings. After years of conditioning at home and school, they don't know how they feel about anything. A very emotional person will be very frustrated and, perhaps, even lose self-confidence in a company where expression of feeling is called "emotionalism." The unemotional person in a volatile and emotional company can be made the butt of every joke which even he or she will understand. Homogeneity of emotional styles leads to fewer people problems. Heterogeneity leads to greater emotional development of everyone. The point here is that a company should be aware of tensions caused by this factor.

Devious and Disrespectful

If your organization is filled with devious people who constantly belittle others behind their backs, you have a problem.

Vicious gossiping and character assassination are the ground-work for company destruction. If your employees cannot develop organization manners, you have a high risk situation. Too much energy goes into nonproductive work. Unfortunately, such a situation can't be eliminated by removing one person. Such behavior is usually a corporate product. Sometimes one or several persons are the agents provocateur. When they can be stopped, usually through separation, it may help. In the long run, however, the problem is one of keeping your organization culture open enough so that such destructive behavior will be nipped in the bud.

In conclusion, the whole population has distributed within it actual pathologies, screwy values, laziness, and personality problems. As a manager the more you have of these problems collected under one roof, the less likely the chances are for your internal processes to work effectively and the lower the odds for your success. Find out by studying the checklist on your company's health and competence.

THE GOAL: THE RIGHT ORGANIZATIONAL CLIMATE

People are an important aspect, but so is the climate in which they function. Real plans, high motivation and good decision making toward agreed-upon goals, open sharing of necessary information, and appropriate distribution of people happen when there is a healthy and competent staff. But people do need an organizational climate where there is minimal risk for them to

— Tell it like it is to each other laterally and vertically.
— Accept openly the help of others without "me-up/you-down" relationships or fear of looking foolish.
— Be different from each other without fear of reprisals.
— Share responsibilities for organizational results.
— Share more of their personal aspirations and covert plans.

In order to decrease the risks around planning, controlling, communicating, and organizing, you can establish a climate where people can be more open, more human, and more cooperative without being put down.

The typical company problem related to this is best illustrated

Check Your Company's Health and Competence

	Yes	No	Unknown
Are the middle managers generally low risk takers?	_____	_____	_____
Is the climate one of cynicism?	_____	_____	_____
Are your people achievement oriented?	_____	_____	_____
Is alcohol a problem for your company?	_____	_____	_____
Are drugs a problem for your company?	_____	_____	_____
Are your people generally competent for today's job?	_____	_____	_____
Do you have many people who are devious or who can't trust others?	_____	_____	_____
Are people excessively devious and disrespectful of others?	_____	_____	_____
Are there long-standing grudges?	_____	_____	_____
Are people willing to do things that are against the law or their conscience?	_____	_____	_____

in the Memo to Management sent by some engineering employees. Of course, there is no such thing as they have requested under Point 2, no-risk communications channels. The request is simply a symptom of the organizational problem, which is a lack of an approved risk-taking climate within the organization. Employees, therefore, in an effort to be heard and to matter to management, and sensing an adversarial relationship, demand an advocate. Their attempt is one possible way to try to change the climate. Let's assume for the moment that there are the same feelings of impotence related to the work itself, that they aren't influencing each other that much either. If that is true, then the time for finding ways to alter the people or the air they breathe has arrived.

There are many theories about improvement programs, ranging from the hatchet men of some management consulting firms to the know-it-all attitude of the do-it-yourself manager. The approach I'm suggesting is a self-help program, enlisting the aid

Memo to Management

Issue:	Management/Employee Communications
Objectives:	To improve and allow for communications between management and employees without recriminations against the latter.
Background:	Many professional employees have expressed resentment and a feeling of isolation as a result of their inability to provide inputs or influence decisions regarding personnel policies. The attempt to solve this problem with the employee relations program has not been sufficient.
Recommendations:	1. Appoint "employee advocates" to serve on the employee relations program committee line. These individuals would present and defend the employee position on such matters as changes in benefits and personnel policies.
	2. Provide effective, no-risk communication channels from engineers to division and group management. The individuals serving as employee advocates could provide an effective personnel communication channel with feedback.

of a behavioral science practitioner. It is a wide collection of theories and various technologies, called organizational development (OD). My definition of OD is: A planned and sustained effort by management to apply behavioral science to organizational practices with the intent of reducing unnecessary personal and financial risks caused by people within the same organization. Properly applied, the result is greater productivity and more effective and satisfying use of human and material resources.

There are already extensive and well-written descriptions of the management philosophy implied and various techniques that can be used to achieve these goals. (See the OD reading list at the back of the book.) I don't intend to duplicate these writings here. I do hope to convince you that the goals of organizational development, as described in my risk-taking framework, should be your goals, that a move toward openness and greater cooperation should be the direction of your organizational change.

THE TOOL: THE REB TAXONOMY
APPROACH TO ORGANIZATION DIAGNOSIS

You have assessed your people. You have decided to move toward more openness and a more human climate. Now you need a tool to let you know how close you are to what you want and what you need to change to get there. I am suggesting a tool, and I am suggesting a few steps to help you get that tool utilized in your organization without getting you fired for meddling.

The first step toward this approach is a risk in itself. The manager with some autonomy must decide to reduce current risk levels in the organization by entering at least a diagnostic phase of an organizational development program. I said with "some autonomy," because you must be autonomous to some degree to be able to take your own risks. If you don't have that authority, then you had better work on your boss or someone on the level above you who does have some. Lacking authority and proceeding anyway will land you in front of the boss, who will probably see you as spending money and time on unnecessary activities.

How do you convince the boss? Convince the boss before you start. Later is almost, although not always, too late. A middle manager who has no budget or relative independence can often do no more than bring this book to top management and say, "Why not us?" This chapter may give you a vehicle to express your concern and to offer a beginning solution to the people problems in your organization that cause frustrations and prevent getting the job done.

Previously, I mentioned getting professional help from a behavioral scientist, either from your own company or from outside. Sometimes these people are hiding in personnel or training offices. They've been trained for years to help, but no one ever asked them. They are like dry wood that's been collected over a period of time. If the manager sets a match to them, he'll be surprised to discover the talent and energy many have. On the other hand, if no one can do it inside, then you have to go outside the company. Don't hesitate, especially for this first try. You need the best. You'll pay through the nose, but you won't regret it. To enter such a process with an amateur is an unnecessary risk.[7]

Once you have decided to move forward, a good consultant can set up a process something like the one I'm including here, called the REB taxonomy approach to organization diagnosis. What I'm about to suggest is sketchy, because your organizational development consultant will have his own approach. Mine is only one of many potential ways to begin. Table 6 is an outline of the phases of this approach. The balance of the chapter spells out the phases in greater detail.

Phase 1: Introduction and Objective Setting

Several possible objectives for an organization diagnosis are listed below. They are neither comprehensive nor mutually exclusive. They are suggested merely to help the manager and consultant focus on the desired outcomes of a diagnostic step.

— To begin a long-range risk reduction effort.
— To take an overall picture of the organization, including the perceptions of the people who work in it and interact frequently with it (as noted in Chapter 9).
— To gather more information and uncover suspected problems for resolution, where possible.
— To audit the company in a way that differs from organization charts, mission and function statements, or resource allocations.
— To provide a mechanism for gaining greater involvement

Table 6. *REB taxonomy approach to organization diagnosis.*

	WHO IS INVOLVED	THE TASK
Phase 1 Introduction and objective setting	Manager and consultant(s)	Decisions on objectives and which associates are to be involved.
Phase 2 Taxonomy modification	Manager, associates, and consultant(s)	Brief explanation by manager to staff. Refining of the framework (taxonomy) from which to gather information.
Phase 3 Information collection	Consultant(s) and people to be interviewed	Information to be collected and collated according to the agreed-upon taxonomy.
Phase 4 Organization diagnosis (diagnostic workshops)	Manager, associates, and consultant(s)	Diagnosis by management team based on the information collected; action steps to be determined.
Phase 5 Action steps	Manager, associates, and consultant(s)	Decisions on action items and further steps to be taken by the manager and staff.

and teamwork in the overall management process, rather than just a concern with a program area or a particular section.

— To provide a common language for people to better understand and discuss how the company functions and what some of its problems are.

- To provide baseline data on the state of the company's health and its stage of development.

- To institutionalize a mechanism by which the company can reassess itself periodically.

- To assist in the rapid orientation of a new boss to what's really happening in the company.

The manager directs the effort. He calls the shots at every major phase of the effort with the consultant there to provide assistance. This means that the manager must be willing to devote substantial time and attention to the taxonomy. In one company where all five phases occurred in one week, the manager devoted 55 percent of his time and key staff some 45 to 50 percent.

Before you go to Phase 2, be sure to give your consultant a chance to sense what kind of an organization you have before you start the process. Let her observe groups at various organizational levels exchanging information, solving problems, and making decisions. Let her talk to managers and staff alike. Let her watch you in action and give you some feedback on how congruent your behavior is with what you say you want.

Phase 2: Taxonomy Modification

The taxonomy, which simply means a systematic classification, is the set of environmental factors, internal processes, and people concerns that your organization has. Chapters 13 and 14 have example categories with checklists after each. You would, with your consultant, choose those basic areas of concern you want examined for excessive risk. The consultant will have suggestions too.

After a taxonomy has been chosen, the next step is to decide who should be interviewed by the consultant and who should be present at the diagnostic workshop, beyond those reporting directly to the manager. Usually the manager will call together those who report to him to review the first draft of a taxonomy so that it generates the desired completeness, specificity, and breadth of information. At this meeting the manager should indicate to the group his objectives for the undertaking, his role, the consultant's role, and the tasks he is assigning to the staff. The group then begins to participate in the effort and shares in its future management. They will decide what key people should be interviewed. Also they will most probably be the group who attends the diagnostic workshop.

The group to be interviewed should include people who run the everyday operations of the company and who are perceived as decision makers, although key staff and key project managers may be involved. The distinction is significant. An undertaking spearheaded by the top person and managed by those next in the hierarchy is more likely to succeed as a serious and integral part of the organization's management, and it is more likely to generate the necessary interest and commitment from the entire organization.

Phase 3: Information Collection

The consultant then carries out the interviews. Each interviewee will have been informed by the management of the diagnostic effort, and will have received a copy of the finalized reporting and interviewing format prior to the interview. Thus, the basis of the interview will be understood and therefore less threatening before the interviewee greets the consultant. OD consultants most often conduct the interviews in an open-ended fashion, letting the interviewee determine the direction although also encouraging the expression of feelings, too. Interviews may be an hour or an hour and one-half, depending on the intensity of concerns, or how much people try to be polite and not tell the truth.

Phase 4: Organization Diagnosis

The actual information gathered from the interviews is placed under taxonomy headings: (1) untouched, raw data, that is, quotes, and where necessary paraphrases which capture meanings that words alone cannot convey; (2) determined by the weight of the concern as sensed by the consultant; (3) sometimes contradictory where there are obviously contradictory views; (4) limited in quantity by the judgment of the consultant regarding what seems appropriate to the representation of the organization's practices and the circumstances under which the diagnosis is to take place. That information which doesn't seem to fit in the taxonomy but still seems of vital interest is included in a special section. This is the taxonomy approach. Your consultant may have her own successful way of getting the same goal, so pay attention to her. This chapter is a cue sheet, not a blueprint.

The manager obviously depends on the consultant to have good judgment, sensitivity, and skill in presenting the right amount of appropriate, unscreened information. Often he must take on faith that the consultant can perform. If the manager has doubts after meeting the consultant, these doubts should be expressed early in the relationship and the go decision be reconsidered. Unless objections or the managers' negative intuitions are satisfactorily dealt with, the risks on continuing are too great for everyone. One way to increase openness is to do it with the consultant.

In order to have adequate time and focused energy for the diagnosis, the manager and the team should set aside a minimum of two days and evenings to analyze the information and begin action steps. Actually, three are much better. The three-day session is best done without interruption and, where not considered strange or disruptive, nights spent together in the same location, away from headquarters, also improve the general climate of the workshop. Where overnight scheduling is impossible, late hours together around food and libation in a hotel meeting room, conference room, or otherwise neutral setting is the next best choice.

Such a diagnostic workshop should be attended by the manager and key subordinates who have a multiplier effect in the organization. In other words, an engineering department meeting should certainly include a specific project manager, who, while not a general manager, has responsibility for the largest project in the department. This group should, of course, be designated quite early, and should not be changed or added to after the process begins. Unless participants have been involved from the beginning, strong people can distort the results out of frustration at not understanding the process or at not feeling proprietorship of the information.

The diagnostic task is to examine the interview data and try to ascertain and list for further discussion the underlying causes of operation difficulties. Generally, diagnosing the entire report for causes is suggested, rather than problem solving too early. Interlocking and overlapping of causes can be determined only when the entire report is examined. One scans the information and looks for underlying reasons rather than focusing on the obvious or the specific. The risks in the company's future lie in these unknowns. The job here is to diagnose what the causes are and attack them.

During this process the consultant can be expected to help the group look at its own communication processes, especially noting where the data in the report seem to be upheld by the actual behavior of people in the diagnostic workshop. For example, the consultant may compare the indirectness of the group's ability to deal with differences and conflict in the group with its tendency toward dealing with conflict in the plant through memos with copies to the boss.

After the group has completed the diagnosis, it will want to tackle what can be solved at that time and plan procedures for removing long-term impediments. At least a day of the workshop needs to be dedicated to this activity. Those managers of a strong problem-solving turn of mind are not favorable toward simply discovering problems or turning over rocks. They want corrective actions, and will judge the success of the workshop on how much follow-through occurs as a result. While their need is not to be overlooked, I have found that the diagnostic process itself often opens up alternative behavior for managers which they adopt individually.

Phase 5: Action Steps

After the workshop is over, together the manager and consultant will review the results. The organization may well have only the normal problems of a healthy, growing company. (Now that they know them, managers can pretty well handle growing pains, and most probably only a yearly checkup will be necessary.) If serious problems between people or groups emerge, then specific OD designs can help. Some top managements are fearful of the words "behavioral science" and "organizational development." For their benefit, I call specific OD techniques on-the-job training. These include, with many others cited in Fordyce and Weil,[8] the following:

Problem	*On-the-Job Training*
A manager's behavior is not congruent	Personal consultation from consultant
Intergroup conflict situation causes potential losses	Intergroup team building
Supervisors and subordinates are not working together well	Team building
Lack of clear objectives	Setting objectives for the organization, the team, and the individual
Roles are unclear	Role negotiation

Basically, there should be a one- to three-year plan developed with specific problems fitting into the development plan. Managers often have to start such a process when the company is experiencing excessive internal troubles. Preventative attention to organizational climate and interpersonal effectivness are, however, the best measure. Few OD people today will do a diagnostic intervention unless the client will consider a development plan that solves problems, prevents new ones, or creates processes by which new ones can be worked more creatively.

Finally, a word of caution: If there is a lack of trust among those at the diagnostic workshop at the end of the taxonomy approach, or if there is excessive evidence of incompetence and defensiveness, management will have other tasks to perform before serious development can begin.

Chapter 14 deals with assessing your staff, the climate in which they operate, and the areas in which organizational change would make them happier and more productive human beings. Eight areas to take into consideration when checking staff health and competence were listed.

You need a balance of green visors and daredevils. You need to keep Pollyannas and bad-mouthers to a minimum. Get a balanced team with different motivations of achievement, power, and affiliation. Stay away from excessive use of mind-altering chemicals. Retrain the obsolete personnel. Don't choose haters, the supercool, or devious people; when you have them, help them to find other outlets for their invidious skills.

After assessing your staff, review the checklists in Chapters 13 and 14 to see whether you need to change your organization's risk-taking style. If so, one approach is that of organizational development, an application of behavioral science to management's need to minimize the cost of risk taking. This approach suggests that the proponent manager must be relatively autonomous, or must convince his boss to try it. A consultant must be acquired and a diagnosis made with the manager's immediate associates. While noting that such a diagnostic phase can have a problem-solving component, another wider implication was described. For a full risk management program, a long-term commitment must be made by management. This chapter presents only the first step.

15 | An Entrepreneurial Team Approach

As NOTED in Chapter 4, groups are subject to the phenomenon called risky shift. This chapter focuses on an alternative to our present use of human resources that takes advantage of the risky shift by creating an entrepreneurial team structure that permits greater sharing of risks and rewards among colleagues. While the alternative I'm suggesting is not the be-all or end-all, it takes into consideration the dilemma for management of large companies especially, but also of many smaller ones, of how to maintain these giants and yet create the same spirit, drive, creativity, risk taking, and devotion to corporate goals often found in the small firm.

Today's large company often faces the problems of lack of real commitment, avoidance of responsibility and risk taking, lack of objectives, destructive competition among executives, poor communication, loss of young managerial talent, and stodgy, demanding unions. It meets these problems with expensive dollar-incentive programs, bonuses in the form of company-paid trips or gifts, profit-sharing plans, and motivational training—none of which provides the "call of the wild" for younger employees.

While the approach described here is organizationwide, it certainly could be modified and tried in a middle manager's area of responsibility. The middle manager interested in trying such a model will need the boss's O.K., the commitment of subordinates, and the cooperation of the personnel department. Sometimes personnel directors are not very open to experimentation of this sort, which means it is important to be prepared to protect their vulnerability as much as possible. Also, your staff may be apprehensive. If you decide to try it, or a modification of it, don't jam it down their throats. Give them time to work with the idea and to influence its application.

Top management is, of course, primarily interested in profitable profit centers. The small team of competent and cooperating co-workers, possessing the same general objectives and having a finite quantity of resources to draw upon, has got to be the best possible profit center ever devised. For example, a small company may rise on the genius of one man's creative ideas, but someone has to develop those ideas. Someone has to market them. Someone has to keep books and pay taxes. As a result, the genius soon has a team: a small group of excited, overworked, usually underpaid people, taking the risk that they will have a product for a yet unknown market and will receive unknown personal rewards.

This company, then, as it succeeds, hires more people. Team members become vice presidents of this and that, and the new employees do the work they once did. As the company grows and continues to succeed—reaping the benefits of the earlier team's risks, sacrifices, and skills—the number of employees so increases that they soon neither know nor care who the genius is or how the company got started. The vice presidents now divide the company into several profit centers, trying to recapture the early days. But now there are 5,000 employees and complex systems of employment, training, production, organization, marketing, and distribution administered through procedures and management structures developed by industrial psychologists in the 1930s—all aimed at servicing and using the individual as the basic profit or cost center.

Somewhere, somehow, the original dream was lost. The employees now see themselves, and are seen, as individuals who are selected, trained, transferred, promoted, rewarded financially, pampered, or blamed by an impersonal corporation. This is quite unlike the early team experience where the indi-

	Two Sets of Management Principles	
Factor	Entrepreneurial Management	Conventional Management
Basic contributing unit	Work group (teams)	Individual manager or employee
Approach to hiring	Potential contribution and fit in work teams	How he measures up as "good" manager or employee
Compensation	Primarily to work groups, secondarily to individual	Primarily to individual, secondarily to groups
Supervision	Collegial supervisory process	One-on-one of individuals in relation to their work
Training	Work groups and individual manager or employee	Individual manager training and some work groups

vidual's personal needs were integrated into the whole, where the team sat down and cried together when things went wrong, worked together 18 hours a day to find a cheaper substance when production cost prevented a healthy profit, shared their victories by getting drunk or simply drooling over the balance sheets. Retirement was eons away! They wanted to taste immediate success, not merely more sophisticated and complicated benefit plans.

This chapter suggests that management needs to take the rather large risk of changing conventional management practices by systematically pushing the concept of profit center to its smallest decimal: a cohesive team. The trade-off for taking the risk is the restoration of the earlier successful model of the enthusiastic team. We shall examine four interlocking personnel functions of management—hiring, compensation, supervision, and training—to propose a change to group-based management, to show how, in part, management has already done it, and to examine the potential problems and risks management faces when it attempts to develop a system based on the group rather than on the individual as the primary organization building block.

HIRING

Under the entrepreneurial team approach, the work group itself (those closest to the job to be done) might interview a prospective team member, or even a proposed supervisor, to ascertain "fit" as well as the competence of the person. This method is used in insurance partnerships and other entrepreneurial enterprises. Perhaps an even better way is to provide a temporary period of employment for the new team member. This trial period would enable the team to have an early opportunity to learn the technical background and feel the personal impact of the prospective member prior to permanent employment. Whatever the procedure, the key point is the team's heavy involvement in the selection process.

If such an approach became a reality within many corporations, most hiring and promotion practices would change. Tests by psychologists and personnel departments would be far less important than the judgment of peer groups. The new responsibility of hiring would make the team more accountable as a team. Perhaps, instead of simply hiring individuals, entire teams from other companies or from other divisions of the same company could be hired or promoted to greater responsibilities. For example, why shouldn't an engineering group, an R&D team, a manufacturing management team, a personnel department team, or a corporate planning team be acquired? This would mean far less time spent training new men; it would provide an organization with a new team ready to produce. Predictability of the team's success would have more reliability than that of a single person whose former success may have depended on his former colleagues more than himself.

How You've Done It Already

Has your company acquired a new company? If so, did it fire all the old management? Probably not, especially if the company was successful. It saw a management team and knew better than to disturb it. Hasn't it hired a chief engineer and gotten two of his associates from the other company? Did you take your secretary with you when you received your last promotion, because you "couldn't do without her"?

If you are a smart manager, you'll look about and discover that informally, and probably unsystematically, you are encouraging combinations of people to stay together when they are productive and involved with one another. You or top management may well resist moving a highly productive person because she is the keystone of a functioning team. This proposal envisions planning for teamwork by creating the circumstances that systematically encourage it rather than simply approving it when it happens.

Potential Problem-Risk Analysis

You may start a trend in your industry and find your best teams raided by the competition. Therefore, the burden is on you to keep in touch with your teams and see that their needs are being met. If they are meeting company needs, the company owes them something and they know it. You may lose certain potential employees who would have worked out well if given a chance by a team. But the converse is also true.

COMPENSATION

Under the entrepreneurial approach the team would increasingly share in the compensation functions of its supervisor. Group compensation would be emphasized. In many companies, basic compensation for each person may well continue to be determined by the personnel department on a companywide basis, using industrywide data on the market value of the basic skills called for in the position.

Raises, however, would be handled differently. At the present time the supervisor is usually given the responsibility of determining performance criteria and distributing the percentage increase received for salaries in the department. Under the entrepreneurial approach, these functions would be assumed by the team. Thus a team would be told the dollars available for raises, and then determine who should get how much and on what performance criteria.

As the team matures and becomes increasingly synergistic around its performance criteria, it would distribute bonuses or participate in cost-reduction plans such as the Scanlon plan formulas or the Rucker share-of-production plan for hourly workers. Bonus plans might be for group performance alone, as is the case for athletic teams in championship playoffs. This procedure would replace top management's present custom of handing out bonuses on an individual basis without having adequate information as to who actually has contributed what. The team knows who did what.

The entrepreneurial team approach also implies that the team ultimately would deal with the problem of decreases of available salary monies within the corporation, such as happened in many industries during 1970–1971. In other words, the supervisor would have no opportunity to secretly recommend to upper management who should be cut from the employment list. The team, with the supervisor, would accept the problem of how to deal with the cut in available salary money. It may decide to take reductions across the board. It may suggest alternatives management hadn't thought of, find new contracts, or even suggest who should leave the team.

As to how much secrecy would be maintained regarding compensation, entrepreneurial teams offer a compromise. Among team members there would be complete openness regarding compensation, including that of the supervisor. Team salary budget data would be available to other colleagues, but the privacy of the individual's compensation would be protected by the group from other teams in the company.

Of course, other factors beside money motivate good teamwork: the desire for a more trusting work climate and the needs for more effective communication and for gaining greater self-confidence. But these lack the wallop that the pursuit of a common survival goal such as common compensation has on building a team. Under the entrepreneurial team system the individual won't be secretly compensated, encouraged to rise above his fellows, and subtly, or not so subtly, told how much better or worse he is performing than those with whom he works daily. He would be trained to recognize that his dollar is in the other guy's pocket. This fact is so obvious in the small partnership accounting firm but so abstract in the large corporation.

How You've Done It Already

When you give your daughter and her friends five dollars for doing the lawn and they decide how to divide it, you have contributed to group compensation. They must decide who should get how much and for what. All you demand is results.

Executive bonuses approach group compensation. The various formulas used by every company always include a formula that is based, in part at least, on a return on assets for the company. While profit-sharing plans are supposed to meet the needs of the nonexecutive, they never have the impact that the executive cash-in-hand bonus has on performance. Why is it that we don't understand that what motivates a vice president also motivates a middle manager as well as a foreman? Partners in firms also realize that when equal compensation and bonuses are simply based on group performance, each person feels called upon to both assist and correct his colleagues.

Potential Problem-Risk Analysis

Under the entrepreneurial team approach you risk losing the competitive motivation of individual against individual. The trade-off is the expected benefit of a highly cooperative relationship which may not motivate certain individuals as much as beating out their neighbors.

There is a possibility that a man may consistently be treated unjustly by his team, especially if they are jealous of his abilities or resentful of his extra efforts. However, this risk is present to an even greater extent in a one-on-one reward system.

Certainly, there are legal limitations in the manpower field which could block implementation of group compensation for hourly workers. Unions would have to be convinced that this approach was not simply a new way for management to squeeze a little more commitment for fewer dollars. This will be difficult to accomplish, for unions have worked hard to create national labor laws to prevent exploitation of employees. The self-interest of the employee, and perhaps the unions themselves, would clearly have to be served by the proposed changes. New plans similar to the Scanlon plan, where employees share in the savings they produce, need to be devised for larger companies.

The entrepreneurial team approach to group compensation does increase the difficulty of orderly control of compensation records. Taxes and other deductions become more complex to record and to project. However, most large companies today have EDP systems often sitting idle. The use of these computers and related equipment can indisputably result in a vastly expanded capacity for accomplishing complicated clerical and administrative operations associated with highly personalized wage benefit plans.[1] So the problem is less mind-boggling than at first glance.

It may also be true that intramural competition between teams will tend to increase, but this competition, if managed with understanding, can contribute to greater motivation.[2] On the other hand, competition between individuals in the same section, which is presently more often the case, is always more difficult to control and can be counterproductive and personally destructive.

SUPERVISION

With entrepreneurial teams is the assumption that supervision becomes everyone's business with accountability being at the door of the entire team. This proposal is almost heretical, for during the last 50 years business has arbitrarily labeled some people management and everyone else workers, technicians, or employees.

In contrast, this proposal implies that there is one class with different functions. For example, it is evident that in more recent years the education and technical competence of personnel in many companies have steadily closed the gap between the presumed all-wise supervisor and her employees. Today's employees are more colleagues than employees; the day of the supervisor knowing how to do everything better than any of her subordinates is certainly passed. No one class of people is responsible for outcomes and processes. Rather, for satisfaction and long-term productivity, everyone must see the job of supervision as his own.

Certain kinds of policy decisions and corporate goals may be established at differing levels of organization. However, when team members are given responsibility for the supervisory process which directs their daily activities, they can seriously affect decisions made by others in the corporation. They will affect company policy when they take active, obvious, and creative risk-taking responsibility for outcomes in their own direct sphere of influence.[3]

A second assumption in this approach is that the designated supervisor is the supporter and facilitator of the management process and the team's formal link with higher management. She isn't a collie dog to nip the heels of the reluctant, recalcitrant sheep. She sets boundaries, communicates overall corporate goals, coordinates, tests the reality of propositions, and acts as consultant to her project managers, thus helping the team to greater productivity and personal satisfaction. The team, including the supervisor, manages the output of its section. The supervisor is a primary resource, but supervisory functions are shared. The concerns of management, for example, quality ideas and production, low overhead, and good selling abilities, are the responsibilities of the entire team, not just of the supervisor.

I'm not suggesting the abdication of management, denying the need for leadership, encouraging the lowering of standards, or any of the other characteristics sometimes unfairly associated with the "soft approach" of Theory Y. Rather, the essential task of management under this approach is to arrange organizational conditions and methods of operation so that people can achieve their own goals best by directing their own, and joint, efforts toward organizational objectives.

How You've Done It Already

The chances are only slight that you have participated in a synergistic work group where the boss and his talents are totally integrated with the talents of his team. More often, you have probably participated in pseudodemocratic groupiness where false harmony and conflict-avoidance persist. Or you've been in organizations that operate under the illusion that they hire the best individuals, and then "adopt a Voltairean stance of allowing them to 'cultivate their own gardens.' "[4] Neither style is what entrepreneurial teams advocate.

The organizational structures that demand the highest synergism from its members are groups under a great deal of stress such as families in crises, small companies struggling to survive, or a football team on a Sunday afternoon. The best description of a synergistic team I have read is Tom Alexander's of the new teamwork between NASA and its contractors forged by the Apollo capsule fire in 1967, in which three astronauts lost their lives. He says

> Suddenly everything changed; the white hot, oxygen-fed flame of the capsule seared its way into the emotions of people in Apollo, cauterizing old differences and forging a wholly new attitude that reached far beyond the technical steps taken to prevent a recurrence of fire. . . . Frequently, now, the government and corporate participants in Apollo display an emotional comradeship that seems unique in industrial life.[5]

Perhaps you've been on such a team.

Potential Problem-Risk Analysis

A potential risk is that top management will lose the kind of "you must do this" authority it now has when dealing with an individual, for groups have more collective power. More negotiation will have to take place between top management and its reporting teams when fundamental changes are sought that involve the judgment of a whole team rather than that of just one supervisor. This need to negotiate may slow down the decision-making process, the last thing needed in today's marketplace. Therefore careful safeguards would have to be devised to protect both the ultimate responsibility of top management and the integrity of a particular team.

TRAINING

With entrepreneurial teams, team training would be emphasized. Rarely would individuals be sent to specialized training.

For example, new personnel would be trained by the team on the job. Time would be specifically set apart for this activity.

The company would spend money mainly to develop an internal team of specialists who would be on hand to help work teams. Outside consultants would be used as resource people for planning or training internal specialists, or for working directly with certain groups in the company. These internal specialists would work with senior management groups, business unit groups (for example, a plant management staff), staff groups (engineering and marketing), project managers and their teams, sales groups (divisional sales manager), administrative groups, and production line teams. Periodically, some of these groups would be pulled out of "doing the job" for a look at "how" they are doing the job in an all-day critique or a weekend meeting in an off-site setting.[6]

The trainer also would attend decision-making–problem-solving meetings of a group to better understand its training needs. He could help the group deal with concerns of its members that may be affecting their work, such as fear of openness and unspoken but destructive interpersonal conflicts.

The specialist would be introduced into a work group when its members feel they need to get the job done better. Hence, if they focus on communication skills, it's because they are having trouble getting along with each other. If they desire sales training, it's because they need new contracts. If they need to understand intergroup conflict, it's because they can't get along with another group with whom they must collaborate.

But the specialist in this system works on their turf most of the time, not they in his classroom. He generally attends their think sessions rather than they attending his courses. The group, not the individual manager, is the corporation's basic educational unit in this approach.

Because, with entrepreneurial teams training is directly related to the problems of the entire work unit and not to the individual employee, there is a realistic and immediate transfer of learnings to daily relationships and work habits. Therefore, the transfer of learning problem, usually associated with training people, is greatly reduced, and behavior changes are immediately applied. Of course, in those cases where the team, or in some cases where the individual, sees a need to develop specific technical, organizational, or human relations skills, provision would be made for individual attendance.

This is not unlike the small insurance agency group of partners and employees which makes a joint decision to send one person to learn about risk management, another to be trained for mutual funds, and yet another to discover the ins and outs of mass marketing. Upon their return, they train others on the job.

How You Are Already Doing It

You may already have a trainer working with a group on how it can increase the effectiveness of its proposal writing. This is, of course, the entrepreneurial team approach. Have you brought in a materials expert when R&D couldn't find what the problem was? Did the expert work with the group? Then, he trained them. Do your work groups plan their objectives together with help from an internal consultant? The unit of training, then, is the group, not individuals.

Potential Problem-Risk Analysis

Perhaps people who have special learning needs will feel they can't ask for special treatment. Quite possible. In fact, likely, for some teams will be less ambitious as teams than some key individuals within those teams. Supervisors will have to be coached on giving such ambitious people guidance toward individual career development tracks within the corporation.

Can a person who doesn't like what he's doing, or whose position becomes less necessary, be retrained for other teams? Certainly, for there would still be individually oriented training courses. But these courses would be the exception, and the target of educational change would always be clear.

If, under present training practices, there is little transfer of learning to the job, wouldn't there be some new problems in this entrepreneurial team approach? Yes. But the problem is of a different order. The problem now will be the natural resistance of groups toward any proposed change. The same forces that ordinarily provide stability and predictability in the work group, when challenged, become the forces that resist any change.[7] For example, a team might be accustomed to meeting only quarterly to solve problems. Their personal work might be geared to such a schedule. A new proposal from a trainer that suggests a need to meet monthly or weekly could raise many objections, no matter how valid the proposed schedule might be.

This chapter has suggested that to regain the bygone entrepreneurial spirit the large company can systematically push the already demonstrably successful concept of profit center to its smallest decimal, the organic team, thus capitalizing on the strengths of the middle manager. The conventions of the recent past, where organization theory has focused almost exclusively on the individual as the main building block, must be challenged.

I've suggested that if companies move as rapidly as possible toward new hiring, compensation, supervisory, and training practices consistent with entrepreneurial team concepts, the result will be the creation of success-oriented teams of corporate radicals. For if management desires greater motivation in corporate life, then we may well need to change the weaving and, perhaps, even the loom on which corporate life has been painstakingly woven.

Perhaps the factor that offers the most comfort to a manager anticipating the change to an entrepreneurial team approach is that people, in general, want their work world to be a place where they can influence as well as be influenced. The Likert studies, as well as my own, show that people generally want a system of management with maximum communication, shared leadership, shared decision making, synergistic goals in which everyone is involved, as well as opportunities for quality production and personal responsibility. The result is shared risk and higher productivity. Management needs only to take the relatively low risk of releasing these forces through entrepreneurial teams, and then help employees develop the structures, skills, and sensitivities within the system

16 | Intergroup Negotiation Strategies

So OFTEN, a manager says, "I can't imagine what's wrong with that division." Perhaps the engineering chief is complaining that manufacturing never follows the specs. Certainly we all expect sales to complain about the poorly kept schedules of manufacturing. The controller will always fuss that sales gives the product away. And so the story of internal strife continues, ad nauseam. Sometimes it is almost fun, like the saying that a bitching outfit is a good outfit. Much of the time, however, the squabbling is energy sapping and destructive of cooperative behavior that could lead to mutual assistance and less costly risk taking.

The problem is often more complex than these simple statements suggest. For example, one beer company had divided its sales and marketing departments. The marketing vice president, who had been quite successful in building a marketing department, was, under a new president, replaced by a less assertive subordinate. Subsequently, the marketing man was made vice president of sales. Sales was, of course, directly affected by marketing creativity. In such a marketplace as that of beer, the products are so similar that the biggest differences are in distribution and packaging practices but, above all, in successful advertising.

Sales began to fall. The marketing department would not change advertising agencies, although both the national and

211

regional sales managers begged them to. Meetings were held for the sales vice president to hear marketing's latest agency creations. After the presentations the sales vice president was having a heart attack, knowing that these tricks wouldn't come close to the competition's super advertising. The national sales manager talked to the national marketing manager but no good came of it, only more anger from the marketing manager. Perhaps worst of all, the sales vice president felt no support from the president, who, he suspected, kept the weak marketing director because he, the president, really wanted to pull the marketing strings. There was, to put it mildly, an impasse. What could the sales vice president do to change the situation?

If he could get the support of the president, he could probably have a toe-to-toe between sales and marketing, with the president being the arbitrator. The risk is high here because people tend to avoid confrontation and conflict. With the president present, people will also pretend more, with nothing but words expressed. Like reluctant schoolchildren being told they must shake hands and make up, they will go through the motions but their behavior won't change.

Another alternative is to persuade the president to merge the two departments under one head. In this case, if the sales vice president was correct, the president wanted to keep his hand on the wheel, so he would not merge the two. He apparently had little concrete interest in the sales organization or problem. He was, of course, interested in the monthly sales volume.

Another chronic area of intergroup trouble occurs between divisions of the same company. In one aerospace group, one division (A) developed and manufactured and sold a part that was 60 percent of a system developed and sold by a sister division (B). Division B did not have a ready market for its system. Division A had other companies and the Department of Defense (DOD) as buyers for its part. Both were tripping over each other in the marketplace, actually to the point of character assassination of each other.

Other peripheral but important factors included the following: Division A was a development house for the group. As such, it received annual investment dollars from Division B. Divisions A and B had good to moderately good working relationships where parts manufactured by A were less than 35 percent of B's systems. None of those had the situation where the part was as much of the whole as in this case. Division B was undercapitalized and was trying to establish itself in the systems market with the DOD. Division A wanted to become a totally self-supporting division and needed the direct contract dollars that sales of the part would bring it.

This kind of situation is not unusual in modern corporations. It is also true for government agencies. In one agency responsible for assistance to developing countries, two organizational elements are responsible to provide technical expertise to the field. One has direct responsibility to the local American field representatives and to representatives of the local government to provide technical know-how. The other group, an R&D group, has a deeper expertise in such fields as agriculture, education, health, and nutrition, not to mention its extensive connections with universities. However, this R&D group is greatly dependent on the field group that has direct responsibility for technical assistance. The R&D group is seen as an ivory tower trying to plug in excessively sophisticated assistance which men in the field feel are irrelevant to local needs. The R&D group, with its technical depth, has management's charter to develop wide and unique approaches to development, thinking five years ahead. The operating environment of the field organizaton is resistant to such ideas.

In another case, a company in the information processing industry has created an R&D group whose charter is to develop technologies for ten years from now. However, there are few career rewards in this company except for those whose ideas are currently being used. This group has representatives from field divisions, but those representatives rarely are able to give the amount of time expected and originally agreed upon to the project. Why? Because there is little immediate self-interest or divisional interest in what this R&D group does. The result is that the R&D group must spend much of its energy designing ways to transfer a technology or a product because it has no organizational links of any strength to the other divisions, and will only be seen as self-serving when it attempts to influence a product group to try something it has developed.

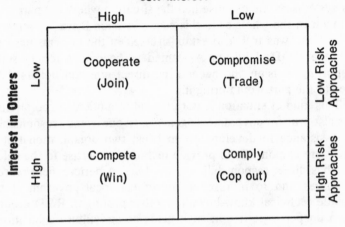

Figure 7. Negotiation strategy matrix.

What, then, are some alternatives when managers get into such binds? Let's look at four strategies and two factors that affect all of them: The first fact is self-interest; the second is interest in others. See Figure 7 for a graphic illustration.

COOPERATION

My concept is not that there should be weaknesses in two departments or divisions in order for them to get along. Rather, true cooperation only occurs when each party is equally invested in protecting its own self-interest as well as that of the other party. In the beer company illustration there was a clear self-interest for both to straighten out the squabble. In the other illustrations the self-interest of each was not clearly served by cooperating with others. The result, then, is a strategy to win.

When one is faced with how to work with another group within one's division, across divisions, or in a team arrangement with another company, the strategy must appeal to the self-interest of all parties. If the problem is yours, then you must work the strategy. The first choice should be joint cooperation because it has the lowest risk for both. The second is trade, or compromise, because it has low risk with potentially good payoff.

The other two, to win (competition) and to cop out (compliance), are both high risk and generally can only hurt the company.

Ideally, cooperation is based not only on goodwill and strategy. If management is wise it is also based on the very way organizations are structured. Over and over I observe that organizations functionally organized by discipline rather than by task are poorly designed to promote cooperation, even though they may promote technical depth. Management needs to build organization structures that suggest when you itch, I scratch. Too often, management expects the nature of people to be brotherly love or mutual exploitation. People in the real world are neither. They are often the result of the lot that is handed them.

Two astronauts in the same cubicle are demonstrably dependent on each other's actions for survival. They will be far more cooperative than, say, two hospitals in the same town, whose cooperation on purchasing one dialysis machine for kidney patients would save the public money. The latter is a rational proposition and an ideal good; the former, a necessity where high personal investment and interdependent results make cooperation a necessity.

Rensis Likert considered structure to be a facilitator of cooperation. In developing a theory of effective organization, he conceived organizations as being composed of groups that act as linking pins.[1] This kind of cooperation, unlike compliance, has low risk. When both parties have something at stake that only their counterparts can make happen, they examine all the factors and peer over each other's shoulder. Therefore cooperation becomes the least risky of all negotiation strategies.

In the beer company illustration, marketing, although an equal organizational unit with sales, could influence sales but sales had no way to influence marketing. Marketing didn't have to listen. Negative results would only show up in the long run, and in this case with the final sale of the company. In the aerospace illustration more organizational strands made each group aware that it needed or at least had to deal with one another's self-interests, both organizationally and from the point of view of career development. It was not in either party's interest to have higher-ups solve the problem. The government agency illustration clearly demonstrated that no matter how much goodwill abounds, "joining" will seldom be the strategy used. Usually, to win will be the first option, with compromise and compliance a distant second.

Competition

Competition between organizational elements happens when both units are highly invested for their own self-interest but have little or no interest in the others. In the beer company example, the sales manager first needs to examine why the marketing manager isn't cooperating. Is it because he feels the sales vice president will swallow him up? Remember, I said he was weaker. On the other hand, if sales go up, isn't it to his department's advantage? Because the situation was as competitive as it was (and I haven't told you the whole story), it seemed to me that both departments were high on self-interest and low on interest in the other department. The result was a competitive situation where each sought to win, rather than a cooperative situation where each had the strategy of "joining."

Competition seemed to be the only option for the aerospace group, until the managers of each, both of them middle managers, designed a way, with outside help, to bring their groups together. The purpose was to examine the factors that made working together, rather than competing, more rewarding. This, of course, is not always possible. There are times when the other party has as its goal the extinction of the other unit, department, or organization; then competition may be a lower risk than either compliance or compromise. When the stakes are clear and the other party is clearly out to do you in, then cooperation is probably not a possibility.

The risks of competition when departments interface are obvious. Each department, by accusing the other of bizarre, irrational, or incompetent behavior, is being destructive of the company's goals. The company continues to lose sales.

The first step toward solving the problem of destructive competition is to do some self-analysis of why the other department doesn't see you as concerned with its interests. These are organizational development techniques that specifically apply to clarifying the motives of the other department or organization.

If the motives are, in fact, misperceived, then a joint cooperative strategy can emerge.

Sometimes changes in structure are all that can alter the competitive situation so that if one person drinks, the other person swallows. Sometimes the risks of competitive destruction can be reduced by groups meeting together with the assistance of a skilled third party to explore why seeking the other person's advantage is advantageous to all. A long conversation sometimes reveals unknown factors, misperceptions, and hurt feelings that block true cooperation and cost the company dollars.

COMPROMISE

The negotiation stance of compromise is sometimes very dangerous. When a department compromises, by its very definition the compromise implies the department has more interest in the other group than it has in its own. Negotiation as arbitration is a popular approach because the idea is that each side gets a little of what it wants and some of what it doesn't want. However, defined in this particular way, negotiation is merely another form of cooperation. In this chapter we mean negotiation to be a less desirable approach because in a cooperative stance each party will be working for and dealing with more than the finite number of possibilities presented in any negotiation process. In other words, there is no synergistic quality that exists with negotiation, as in the cooperative strategy. Negotiation is especially risky when the other party is in a competitive mood. You may give away the cookie jar when it wasn't necessary. Generally, negotiation is most useful when cooperation fails.

In a management competitive exercise for church executives, two of three groups instructed their representatives to vote for the other groups as being the best groups, which they did. There they were, three people sitting in the middle of a room of 35 people. No. 1 rep said to No. 2 rep, "I really believe you have the best group." No. 2 rep said to No. 3 rep, "I think you have the best group." No. 1 rep said, "All right, what's in it for you? I don't believe this."

Perhaps there is more of a compliant attitude here than compromise, but both are present. Where one sees the other group not acting out of its own self-interest, it causes suspicion. Compromise by this definition is certainly risk taking because you are never quite sure that the result was heated and forged enough. A risky situation in business compromises can be avoided if a manager will try to increase the visibility of the self-interest of the other group in the final result. Sometimes structure changes must come from above to do the trick. At other times, again, constructive negotiations with a third party can be of assistance.

COMPLIANCE

The fourth strategy of dealing with other organizational elements is compliance. This strategy is most often used by departments that have given up trying to influence their colleagues or their bosses. In this case an organization may tire of trying to cooperate and compromise because it always loses face and arguments. As a result it simply complies with what it knows is neither in its self-interest nor in the long-term interest of its antagonists.

Thus a safety group in an automobile manufacturing corporation may give up trying to keep its management in tune with potential government constraints. An equal opportunity manager may develop only innocuous compliance programs that finally lose the corporation a large government contract. Defendants in the Watergate case often indicated they had complied. Wasn't the highest authority behind their action?, they asked.

Compliance in these circumstances always exposes the organization to excessive risk, for top management or other segments of the organization often cannot tell the difference between compliance and loyal behavior, which means they will not understand what the complier is agreeing to. The risks, of course, are the greatest in such a cop-out because the organization is neither acting in its own self-interest or in the interest of others.

Of all the traps for middle management, this is the worst. Middle managers, over 40, fearful of losing their jobs, and sensing they have plateaued, often comply, resulting in their contributing to greater exposure for the company. It is a self-fulfilling prophesy in which middle managers fear they will be seen as a drag and risk for the company, and then act in ways that indeed have the predicted results. Only the middle managers can extricate themselves from such a situation.

The most important part of understanding these strategies is to avoid one consistent style. Some years ago President Moos of the University of Minnesota was accused of permissiveness for not bringing certain radical elements to court for taking over the administration building and causing several thousand dollars worth of damage. He told the legislators that his strategy was never to respond in the same way, but rather to take each situation on its merits and then decide. This seems rational, rather than some ideal position on what strategy one should always use. There is a time to cooperate, a time to compete, a time to compromise, and a time to comply. Each judgment should be based on the factors surrounding the given situation.

In other words, even though you want to cooperate, the other people may not. Even though you want to compete, they may comply quickly. Your self-interest may be served better if they respond in kind with your strategy. What can you do, presuming the other organization's intentions are not your political destruction?

While it takes two to tango, somebody has to ask. Once you understand the dynamics, you can gain a perspective and approach the situation with a third eye. You can approach the other manager and explore in an abstract way the cost-benefit gains to the other organization, playing it your way. Don't discuss the substance of the problem, only the joint strategy to be used. Finally, if you work to create the kind of organizational climate described in Chapter 15, the likelihood of being believed is much greater in any intergroup relationship within your organization.

In this chapter the reader can see the sociodynamics that often exist between organization units. I've suggested that there are four basic strategies you can adopt with these other organizations, depending on the specific issues you commonly face. Cooperation has the lowest risks and potentially the highest payoff because both self-interest and the other group's concerns are the modus operandi. The next least risky is to compromise. However, while compromise takes the other organization's interest into account, truth may not be served except when facts are brought to light by active self-interest publicly displayed. In other words, compromise may avoid conflict and consequently the solution may not be as thoroughly worked out as it should be. The third approach is to compete, which has as its primary motivation one's own interest, not the interest of the other. The fourth strategy is to comply, which really is quite risky because rarely is either party's interest served, except the one of avoiding conflict.

I suggested that organizations preferring the cooperation method should create organizational structures that make it almost always a requirement to cooperate. Then, too, remember that each strategy can be appropriate. Each is applied to a given set of circumstances, and the risk calculated, before a selection is made.

Appendixes

CREATIVE RISK TAKING TRAINING
A New Tool for Human Resources Development

IN THE FAST-MOVING FIELD of laboratory, or sensitivity, training for managers, supervisors, and salaried and hourly employees, much emphasis has been placed on program designs and the adaptations of designs tailored for the needs of specific companies to bring about organizational development. Many criticisms have been made of sensitivity training when the latter has been conceived as composed essentially of T-groups.[1] It is now timely to ask: How useful can instructional laboratories with absolutely no T-groups or structured tools such as the Managerial Grid be as learning experiences? Is there any reason to believe that nonstructured laboratories could surpass structured labs for certain purposes? I believe the answer is clearly affirmative.

After conducting 25 five-day labs for employees of industrial and other organizations during the past several years, it seems that just as the T-group was a quantum leap forward compared to the conference-type design in human relations training, the Creative Risk Taking (CRT) design is still another quantum improvement. In an age in which creativity is on every personnel manager's mind and a potent force on the profit and loss statement, it would seem that people should know about a gimmick-free approach to learning that creatively releases the individual's inner resources and causes him to take both calculated and spontaneous risks. Thus the purpose of this appendix is to present an alternative for the development of human resources through sensitivity (laboratory) training.

WHAT IS A CRT LAB?

Creative Risk Taking is a laboratory learning design born out of a need discovered several years ago in work with administrators and pastors who wanted to become agents of change, that is, prime movers of organizational, interpersonal, and even individual change. Although they wanted change in themselves and in their environments, more often than not they were unable to achieve these aims. For too long they had overvalued one set of responses to life. These included self-control, willpower, self-criticism, caution, measured thought, intellectualized faith, and deliberateness.

The resulting gap between what they said they wanted to change and their actual resistance to change in more group-process-oriented and structured laboratories led to a search for a new learning design. This same design has since been used for a variety of groups, including businessmen, and appears to have its greatest potential among that group, given the fact that we live in an age of complex, large-scale organizations that seem to negate creativity and risk taking.

A laboratory design was sought that would redress the balance of values somewhat in favor of human spontaneity, expressiveness, and trust and less inhibited, unpremeditated, and calculated expression of one's self. For two years a team of trained researchers experimented with a variety of trainer-led experiences, including competitive games and nonverbal exercises, seeking to increase the courage to fail and self-confidence in the interpersonal relations of trainees.

However, it wasn't until the radical shift of putting the responsibility for learning on the participants was made that paydirt was struck. The more learning initiative shifted on them, by withdrawing lecture schedules, T-groups, and other such techniques, the more self-starting and self-directing they became. For most people that meant redressing the balance in favor of risk rather than self-control and of spontaneity rather than deliberateness.[2] Thus we started to see people saying and doing things on their own volition, which they probably would never have done outside the laboratory environment. They were happy, animated, and ready to do some real learning—through their own behavior. Why?

Let's look at the goals of the lab and how they are implemented.

THE GOALS OF THE LAB

The goals of this new laboratory education are greater personal autonomy and openness to new ideas and behavior through being all there (in the here and now), being open (to new ideas), being for real (with other people), and being experimental (with everything). Each of these concepts is worth a few words of explanation.[3]

Being all there implies the fullest use of one's total person in the present moment (that is, in the here and now).

Being open means the state of being relatively nonevaluative of input from one's own inner world as well as from others. It means being disposed not to attach labels and rubrics on feelings, persons, places, and experiences that limit full comprehension.

Being for real is being genuinely and subjectively involved in relationships to the degree your world permits.

Being experimental means acting out, trying out, entering into, and initiating change. It implies self-starting, self-directed, self-motivated, confident, and risk-taking living.

Managers might be scared off by these words at first, but many of those who committed themselves fully at the CRT lab discovered more effective ways of being themselves.

THE LAB ITSELF

The CRT training laboratory is a four- or, ideally, a five-day residential experience sometimes sponsored by a single client organization but most often open to the public. It is called risk taking because the format calls for personal self-directed experimentation as a necessity for social survival during the five days. The lack of given tasks and direction from leaders places the total burden for action on the participant. The *Creative Risk Taking Training Laboratory: Book of Basic Readings,* usually distributed before the participants arrive, stresses experimentation and personal growth, encouraging participants to expect to take personal risks.

But risks can be creative or destructive. We define as creative those risks that lead the participating persons toward greater acceptance of their own latent potential, their inner core, and to respond more appropriately to the demands of each situation. We have found that when they are given the choice, people set personal growth goals that are humanistic and other-centered, not narcissistic and psychopathic. We encourage creative risks because we are committed to an understanding of man that assumes his inner nature is not evil. In fact, the predominance of helpful, responsible behavior which emerges as coping tactics by lab participants would lead one to conclude that risks can never be destructive, although on occasion we see that they are.

The following sections outline how learning that is dependent on traditional educational and training techniques differs from the CRT lab, which is dependent on the environment to bring about behavioral change. Then the format of Creative Risk Taking laboratories is given.

THE TECHNIQUE VERSUS
ENVIRONMENTAL EMPHASIS IN LEARNING

Most of us think of education as a particular set of techniques to induce a particular kind of growth in the student. These techniques include assigned reading, lectures, tests, question-and-answer sessions, audiovisual aids, and the like in conceptual teaching. But those involved in social-emotional education are also committed to learning through other techniques. For example, psychodrama, role playing, nonverbal exercises, trainer interventions in T-groups, and certain types of therapy are important ways that have been developed to induce various kinds of growth experiences.

Still another approach to social-emotional education is environmental manipulation. In other words, we can plan ways to affect the use of time-space dimensions in a learning environment so that we control to a great degree the nature of the experience and the learning outcome. To illustrate, a small living room assures a certain kind of noisy, close cocktail party. Conversely, a ballroom may be a cold, alienating experience. Often there is a lack of emphasis on the learning environment as a direct input for the short-term laboratory experience.

The use of space, time, and expectations makes the difference in what kind of learning experience people will have. Too often, management educators in both traditional and laboratory forms of learning have ignored the proper use of time and space. Dingy factory classrooms, stiff chairs, poor accommodations, and plain food served at training locations and at times inconvenient to the stomach are only a few examples of our inadequacy in taking our environment seriously. Conversely, we often provide management education at unnecessarily plush resorts with unpredicted distracting features created by a vacation atmosphere. The point is that the environments are attendant to hierarchical nuances rather than educational needs.

Creative Risk Taking laboratories are meticulously planned environmental experiences. But it should be stressed that great attention is paid to the environment itself, not only to the techniques the staff will use. Actually, there are 20 specific ingredients of the environment that are carefully planned by the administrators of the CRT lab (although the specific conditions discussed here represent broad descriptive strokes rather than rigid requirements). Let us take a closer look at some of these environmental conditions that make this laboratory different in approach from the more traditional or technique-oriented learning experiences.

SPECIFIC CONDITIONS OF CREATIVE RISK TAKING LABS

The first condition is the elements that are provided.

A given environment of rooms, people, materials, time, and staff and resource people, expert and experienced in the development of human potential.

Usually these elements are available in a first-class motel with double rooms clustered about one or more large meeting rooms. Some equipment and materials are provided. These include art materials, records, and copies of *CRT Basic Readings*. A simple commercially available test inventory of one's personal orientation is completed by lab participants, if they wish [4] (which we discuss in more detail subsequently). Staff people are available to each participant to review the scores on this battery of

self-actualizing variables. Most participants find this review helpful as a benchmark of where they are at and from which they can
consider their CRT behavior.

All these elements comprise a minimal structure for change
induction. In comparison with other sensitivity laboratories,
the CRT lab is structureless. It appears that the fewer the struc-
tural demands made on a person, the more he will spontaneously
reach into himself and become an active agent of his own development.

Anywhere from 15 to 30 people may be in the CRT laboratory. More often than not the participants are of different
sexes, backgrounds, and ages. They are asked not to reveal any
historical data. Even their last names are withheld where feasible.
This total anonymity sometimes threatens and inhibits, but more
often frees people to be more spontaneous. To the extent a person has integrated his roles and his identity, there is very little
concern or anxiety about who does what. Despite the variations
in backgrounds and ages of the participants, they turn out to be
exciting and growth-oriented as a group.

The second condition is a time-space principle of freedom.
The only constrictions are those that are self-imposed.

In other words, no person in authority tells people when they
must start or stop talking, when they must or must not eat, when
to go to bed, when to work, what places any of these things should
be done, what to wear, where to sit, or to whom they must relate.
The only restrictions on time, place, or behavior are those normally enforced by the cultural norms present in a motel with a
liberal policy towards its guests.

The importance of the individual's control of time in self-
development has recently been stressed by Lippitt:

No man experiences time quite the same as another man. Therefore,
more productive use of the time can be achieved only in accordance with
one's self-concept. We should reexamine these things with which philosophy is concerned—not clocks and calendars but values and goals.[5]

CRT labs seem consistent with individual freedom in time control.

In this climate participants suddenly find that their own constrictions are self-imposed. If they want to dance, they may do so. If they want to yell, no one denies them the right. If they want to disappear into their rooms and test their personal tolerance for being alone, they may. If they want to argue, they may. Some organize groups; some avoid groups. A variety of forms of behavior emerges, far more than is manifested in the circle of the T-group.

Whatever they choose to do is modified by what others are doing. This means that the persons who decide to sleep may find someone else working on finding ways to motivate lethargic people. The persons who talk too much may encounter those who are trying to be more candid with their feelings toward big talkers. Thus self-imposed constrictions are the result of negotiated freedom and responsibility. As a result, everyone discovers more clearly his own value system: what is dysfunctional and what is functional for him.

Many persons have fantasies about the evil things they would do if all external constrictions and pressures were removed. However, they soon see that most of their constrictions are really self-imposed. The discovery of new strengths removes the necessity for protection of past weaknesses. The lab gives them an opportunity to sort out the inhibiting values that are harmful and then increases their self-appreciation when they find they as well as others are not capable of as disturbingly evil deeds as they had feared. Such an insight can help managers to loosen up and consider more open, trusting relations with their peers.

Another laboratory condition relates to self-direction.
The only opportunities are the ones you yourself create.
This statement implies everyone must make his own learning experiences. This is true because in CRT no one in authority is planning or implementing another's learning experience. By themselves and with those from whom they request help, persons set their own growth goals or aspirations and then enlist others to assist in achieving them. This aid is accompanied by reciprocity and much candid feedback. However, the environment often appears to be a happy one, and even the most devastating feedback becomes surprisingly acceptable.

Designing their own learning experiences is most difficult when these people feel inadequate. They find it difficult to take charge of their everyday lives. They would like to flee from the world or learn more satisfying coping tactics. They often feel others know what to do, especially the teacher, boss, or authority figure. In the CRT lab they discover that nothing will be achieved unless they seek people out, join activities they want to, leave when they wish, and assertively try out their new ideas and behavior.

Because others in the laboratory are also trying out new ideas, they may even find themselves becoming reactors instead of actors, helping others rather than doing their own thing. The realization that they have become another person's tennis ball or a sounding board for another's ideas while not achieving their own goals often strikes them the second day. This causes a reassessment of how much they should give and how much they should demand for themselves. They may refuse to continue playing such a role and start initiating what they want. They become more spontaneous or controlling, assertive or cooperative, independent or dependent, orderly or "irresponsible." They seek their own peak emotional and intellectual experiences.

Another prime element in the environment is the behavior of the professional staff.

The staff member models risk-taking, growth-oriented behavior in his every activity in the lab.

Staff persons are selected because they themselves are fully functioning persons who are seeking personal growth. Participants are consistently surprised, disbelieving, and delighted (normally, in that order) at the personal investment and openness of staff personnel.

Staff personnel are also selected for their background in applied behavioral science. Usually a CRT trainer has had experience in a variety of laboratory settings. One reason for this policy is to have some people in the group with a basic knowledge of the theory of human behavior who can help participants sort out their growth goals. These qualifications provide a kind of resource any growth environment needs. They in no way act as instructors or as traditional group leaders.

The staff who are trained to discern strikingly dysfunctional behavior are prepared to deal with it when necessary through counsel and confrontation. It has never been necessary to ask anyone to leave a laboratory, although it is possible that a time may come when such action would be appropriate. The staff believes that given a really supportive culture such as the CRT lab provides, the true essence of man is more likely to appear than is destructive, reactive, defensive behavior. In other words, the behavior of most people who have attended Creative Risk Taking labs has confirmed our assumption that people, given the opportunity, work for actualization of their social, not antisocial self. As for the sadist, exploiter, or pervert, I am inclined to agree with Maslow:

> If the sadist, exploiter or pervert says "why shouldn't I express myself?," the answer is that such an expression is a denial of, and not the expression of, . . . (inner core). Each neuroticized need, or emotion or action is a loss to the person, something that he *cannot do* or *dare not do* except in a sneaky, unsatisfying way. In addition he has usually lost his subjective well-being, his will and a feeling of self-control as well as the capacity for pleasure and self-esteem.[6] (italics added)

My experience does not rule out expecting potential problems in the lab or in life. People sometimes do exhibit destructive hostility, generalized fear, and meanness. In the labs, as elsewhere, there are expressions of neurotic needs, emotions, attitudes, definitions, action. But I think these are not expressions of the inner core or real self. In any case the trainer is prepared to deal quickly with such difficulties when they appear in participant behavior.

RESULTS OF CRT LABS

Some real changes take place in Creative Risk Takers that appear to be qualitatively different from changes in participants of more structured laboratories. For one thing, they report a feeling of liberation and call the lab a freeing experience. Managers who are driven by a daily appointment book find the unstructured lab a refreshment and tend to become reflective on their lives there and then, based upon here-and-now experiences. Engineers spend hours listening to music or swimming and take on a happy countenance. Men who are highly rational decision makers find people who help them become less rigid, if not downright playful, in the lab. Somewhat disorganized people struggling to improve get ideas on how to cope more methodically and try out the new systems in the happy ambience of the lab.

In several quantitative studies, the more structured lab (planned T-group sessions, nonverbal exercises, community exercises, and theory presentation) has been compared with the CRT lab. Shostrom's self-administered Personal Orientation Inventory of 150 items pertaining to self-actualization was used for one measurement. Participants in structured labs and CRT labs completed the questionnaire before and three months after training. Creative Risk Takers showed significantly more gains than the participants in the structured lab on five variables: personal autonomy, holding the values of self-actualizing people, expressing feelings in spontaneous action, holding a constructive view of the nature of man, and acceptance of aggression in oneself as natural. Although not statistically significant, differences between Creative Risk Takers and participants in the structured lab on nine other subscales also favored the Creative Risk Takers.[7]

Another measure was used to discover whether the values underlying the training objectives had been translated into actual changed attitudes and behaviors on the job. This was an open-ended, perceived change questionnaire completed three months after training by each subject, a procedure first used successfully by Douglas Bunker.[8] An analysis of the resulting data showed a greater percentage of gains in structured laboratory trainees than in the subjects of Creative Risk Taking in the categories of self-control, awareness of human behavior, acceptance of others, and sensitivity to others' feelings. In contrast, a greater percentage of the Creative Risk Takers showed more positive gains in risk taking, interdependence, and self-confidence.

Of the other variables, participants of both kinds of labs showed larger, positive gains. Especially noteworthy, and similar to results of previous studies, is the marked increase for participants in insight into one's self and role, functional flexibility, and facility in interpersonal relations.

Further evidence needs to be gathered on the usefulness of Creative Risk Taking for individuals and organizations. It would be of interest to discover if all CRT trainees at laboratories tend to have the same hangups or if there is no consistent profile. The hangups of CRT trainees seem to come out of expressed needs to become more autonomous and their ability to deal with life creatively. They come wanting more courage to risk success. They are often tired of being overly sensitive and controlled by their excessive need to be liked by their associates and their supervisors, which limits their ability to produce for the organization.

CONCLUSION

It is not certain which of the many different kinds of organizations will find CRT labs most useful. Today, organizations tend to send people who fit into one or more of the following categories:

- Those whose job involves an extensive time span between action and the results by which their performance can be judged.
- Those desiring personal renewal and creativeness.
- Those whose job is so different as to make it difficult to compare their product with the product of other people in the organization.
- Those who are an integral part of a team where there is no direct connection between their input and the team product.

Obviously many managerial, supervisory, technical, and professional employees fit these categories. The results of early studies suggest that the lab has wide relevance and may be a useful antidote for persons who are feeling excessive bureaucratic constrictions or who are underachieving in organizations of all sizes. This being the case, CRT labs should be of great value to people in a variety of organizational settings. They are certainly a viable alternative to sensitivity training based upon T-groups, and should be given serious attention by personnel managers and organizational development specialists in both private industry and public employment.

AN OD READING LIST

THERE ARE many major and minor theorists in the applied behavioral science approach called organization development. I've outlined briefly the thoughts of ten of them. Each author's application could be seen as a risk reduction strategy. Each has devotees among managers and organization development consultants. A manager thinking of adopting the organization risk reduction strategy should read at least some of these works.

Chris Argyris. *Interpersonal Competence and Organizational Effectiveness*. Homewood, Ill.: Irwin, 1962.

VALUE CHANGE/INTERPERSONAL COMPETENCE
Argyris' basic paradigm is that bureaucratic values tend to stress the rational task aspects of work and ignore basic human factors related to the task. Managers who have adopted these values tend to be inept and anxious in relationships. This leads to mistrust, intergroup conflict, conformity, and rigidity, which interferes with the problem-solving capacity and success of the organization. He suggests certain kinds of change models for improvements.

W. G. Bennis and Philip E. Slater. *The Temporary Society*. New York: Harper & Row, 1968.

A THEORY OF TEMPORARY SYSTEMS OR ORGANIZATION REVITALIZATION
Bennis and Slater have designed a potential 20th century model for organizations as opposed to pyramid arrangements of most organization charts. Bureaucracy has a well-defined chain of command, well-defined procedures and rules for work-related contingencies, division of labor based on specialization, promotion

and selection based on testimonial competence and impersonality in human relations. They propose an organization of "adaptive, problem-solving, temporary systems of diverse specialists, linked together by coordinating and task evaluating executive specialists in an organic flux."

Robert Blake and Jane Mouton. *The Managerial Grid.* Houston, Tex.: Gulf Publishing, 1964.

THE TWO FACTOR GRID RE: MANAGEMENT STYLE AND ASSUMPTION
Blake and Mouton identify five key managerial assumptions based on three organization universals: production, people, and hierarchy. They demonstrate the effect of a manager's orientation on such organization variables as goals, boss-subordinate relationships, approaches to managing conflict, commitment, management development and personal behavior, and what organizational conditions each style promotes.

J. R. Gibb. "Fear and Facade: Defensive Management," in R. E. Farson, ed., *Science and Human Affairs.* Palo Alto, Calif.: Science and Behavior Books, 1965.

TRUST FORMATION
Gibb describes a theory of development that assumes an organization can best be understood and improved by focusing upon growth dynamics. He views growth dynamics as occurring within the four primary concerns—acceptance, data flow, goal formation, and social control. These latent concerns, often camouflaged, are at the manifest level, seen as concerns regarding membership, decision making, productivity, and organization. Growth rate can be directly influenced by emergent management, certain kinds of training, critical events in the macroenvironment, and new experiences of caring, consensus, investment, and emergence.

R. Kahn, D. Wolfe, R. Quinn, S. Snoek, and R. Rosenthal. *Organizational Stress.* New York: Wiley, 1964.

ROLE-SET THEORY
Kahn and associates develop the concept that the behavior of an employee is the product of motivational forces that derive

mostly from behavior of the members of his role-set (his sub-group). Their expectations serve to regulate his behavior. Only when his expectations or those around him are changed through training, renegotiation, or restructuring will the relatively stable role-set change.

P. R. Lawrence and J. W. Lorsch. *Organization and Environment: Managing Differentiation and Integration.* Boston: Division of Research, Graduate School of Business Administration, Harvard University, 1967.

AN INTERFACE APPROACH TO ORGANIZATION IMPROVEMENT
Lawrence and Lorsch use a systems approach to understanding and improving organization. They have developed a model of differentiation and integration that provides the manager with the organization characteristics they think an organization needs in order to perform its particular mission in its particular environment. They suggest four primary concerns: the degree of differentiation, the pattern of integration, integrative mechanisms, and conflict-solving behaviors.

Rensis Likert. *The Human Organization: Its Management and Value.* New York: McGraw-Hill, 1967.

SYSTEMS-BASED MANAGEMENT
"The management system of an organization must have compatible component parts if it is to function effectively," says Likert. He develops a framework which describes four management systems: exploitative authoritative, benevolent authoritative, consultative, and participative group. He advocates a systems approach to management and organization improvement. He also identifies the key to organizational improvement as overlapping group structures (variable: character of organization structure), group decision making (variable: leadership principles employed), and the principle of supportive relationships being applied (variable: major assumptions concerning motivation).

George H. Litwin and Robert A. Stringer, Jr. *Motivation and Organizational Climate.* Boston: Division of Research,

Graduate School of Business Administration, Harvard
University, 1968.

ORGANIZATIONAL CLIMATE EFFECTS ON MOTIVATION
Litwin and Stringer describe key elements in an organization's
climate. They postulate how each of these elements, namely,
structure, responsibility, warmth, support, reward, conflict,
work standards, identity, and risk, affect Atkinson and McClelland's concepts of achievement, affiliation, and power motivations. They then suggest ways in which managers may influence
climate factors to enhance particular motivations.

Douglas McGregor. *The Human Side of Enterprise.* New York:
McGraw-Hill, 1960.

MANAGERIAL ASSUMPTIONS ABOUT MOTIVATION.
THEORY X AND THEORY Y
McGregor analyzes the traditional view of direction and management control which rests on three basic assumptions: (1)
human beings inherently dislike work; (2) people must be made
to perform; and (3) the average person wants direction, little
responsibility, and security above all. He suggests that when
management makes opposite assumptions, the result will be
genuine innovation and the utilization of the potentialities of the
average employee. He examines the effect on specific management actions when either set of assumptions is held.

Abraham H. Maslow. *Eupsychian Management.* Homewood,
Ill.: Irwin–Dorsey Press, 1965.

EUPSYCHIAN MANAGEMENT
Maslow defines eupsychian as the "culture that would be generated by 1,000 self-actualizing people on some sheltered island
where they would not be interfered with." The concept implies
only real possibility rather than certainty or confident predictions of the future. He applies the concept to individuals and organizations and to other theorists' assumptions and values, noting that many relative applications need to be made and offering
a unique perspective on organizations.

References and Notes

Introduction

1. *Work in America* (Cambridge, Mass.: MIT Press, 1972). A report of a Special Task Force to the Secretary of Health, Education and Welfare.
2. Alfred T. DeMaria, Dale Tarnowieski, and Richard Gurman, *Manager Unions?* AMA Research Report (1972), p. 13.
3. L. C. Wynn, I. M. Ryckoff, Juliana Day, and S. I. Hirsch, "Pseudomutuality in the Family Relations of Schizophrenics," *Psychiatry*, Vol. 21, 1958, pp. 205–220.
4. Michael R. Barrett, "Motivating Middle Management," *Plant Management & Engineering*, September 1972, p. 34.

Chapter 1

1. John Gardner, *No Easy Victories* (New York: Harper & Row, 1968), pp. 50, 51.
2. Carl Rogers, *On Becoming a Person* (Boston: Houghton Mifflin, 1961).
3. S. I. Hayakawa, *Symbol, Status, and Personality* (New York: Harcourt, Brace and World, 1958).
4. Karen Horney, *Neurosis and Human Growth, The Struggle Toward Self-Realization* (New York: Norton, 1950).
5. Emanuel Kay, "New Alternatives for Middle Managers," *Management Review*, October 1973, pp. 4–10.
6. Horney, op. cit., p. 35.
7. Nathan Kogan and M. A. Wallach, *Risk Taking: A Study in Cognition and Personality* (New York: Holt, Rinehart and Winston, 1964).
8. Kurt Lewin is perhaps the father of applied social psychology. For information on him, see Alfred S. Marrow, *The Practical Theorist: The Life and Work of Kurt Lewin* (New York: Basic Books, 1969).

236

9. John Lillibridge and Sven Lundstedt, "Some Initial Evidence for an Interpersonal Risk Theory," *Journal of Psychology,* 1967, pp. 119–128.
10. Ibid.
11. For an excellent description of betting on static risks, see Matthew P. Dumont, "Down the Bureaucracy!" *Trans-action,* October 1970, pp. 10–14.

Chapter 2

1. Sidney M. Jourard, *The Transparent Self,* 2nd edit. (New York: Van Nostrand-Reinhold, 1971).
2. David C. McClelland, *The Achieving Society* (Princeton, N.J.: Van Nostrand, 1961).
3. Nathan Kogan and M. A. Wallach, *Risk Taking: A Study in Cognition and Personality* (New York: Holt, Rinehart and Winston, 1964).
4. J. W. Atkinson, ed., *Motives in Fantasy, Action, and Society* (Princeton, N.J.: Van Nostrand, 1958).

Chapter 3

1. The Wilson Center in Faribault, Minnesota, is a psychiatric treatment residential center for adolescents between 15 and 22 who have psychiatric disorders.
2. David C. McClelland, *The Achieving Society* (Princeton, N.J.: Van Nostrand, 1961).
3. Alfred T. DeMaria, Dale Tarnowieski, and Richard Gurman, *Manager Unions?* AMA Research Report (1972), p. 13.
4. Thomas H. Patten, Jr., *Manpower Planning and Development of Human Resources* (New York: Wiley, 1971), p. 712.

Chapter 4

1. R. D. Clark III and E. P. Willems, "Where Is the Risky Shift? Dependence on Instructions," *Journal of Personality and Social Psychology,* 1969, pp. 215–221.
2. N. Bateson, "Familiarization, Group Discussion, and Risk-Taking," *Journal of Experimental Social Psychology,* Vol. 2, 1966, pp. 119–129.
3. D. J. Bem, M. A. Wallach, and Nathan Kogan, "Group Decision Making Under Risk of Aversive Consequences," *Journal of Personality and Social Psychology,* 1965, pp. 453–458.
4. Edwin P. Willems and Russell D. Clark III, "Shift Toward Risk

and Heterogeneity of Groups," *Journal of Experimental Social Psychology,* 1967, Vol. 7, pp. 304–312.

5. R. Brown, *Social Psychology* (New York: Free Press, 1965).
6. Bem, Wallach, and Kogan, op. cit.
7. Dorwin Cartwright, "Determinants of Scientific Progress," *American Psychologist,* March 1973, pp. 222–231.
8. "Interpersonal Risk Scale (IR Scale)," Sven Lundstedt (Ohio State University, 1966).

Chapter 5

1. Alfred T. DeMaria, Dale Tarnowieski, and Richard Gurman, *Manager Unions?* AMA Research Report (1972).
2. This phrase was first used by T. H. Patten to describe the dilemma of foremen. Today it may be more applicable to middle managers.
3. DeMaria et al., op. cit., p. 13. *Note:* Unless indicated otherwise, all quoted material in this chapter comes from this source.
4. Emanuel Kay, "New Alternatives for Middle Managers," *Management Review,* October 1973, pp. 4–10.
5. NLRB, Managerial Employees Sec. 2(2), 9(b), Bargaining Unit, Sec. 9(b).
6. *Work in America* (Cambridge, Mass.: MIT Press, 1972), p. 53.
7. Stuart A. Taylor, "Room at the Top? Not for Blacks," *The New York Times,* January 14, 1973.
8. Ibid.
9. Virginia Schein, "Implications and Obstacles to Full Participation of the Woman Worker," *Best's Review* (Life/Health Insurance edit.), April 1972, pp. 22–68.
10. Marchia E. Hanson, "Women in Leadership Roles at the University of Minnesota," Masters thesis, June 1972, University of Minnesota, Minneapolis.
11. *Work in America,* p. 60.

Chapter 6

1. The first concept is well developed by Sven Lundstedt, "Interpersonal Risk Theory," *Journal of Psychology,* 1966, Vol. 62, pp. 3–10; the second by Sidney M. Jourard, *The Transparent Self,* 2nd edit. (New York: Van Nostrand-Reinhold, 1971).

Chapter 7

1. William H. Whyte, Jr., *The Organization Man* (New York: Simon & Schuster, 1956), pp. 276–277. With permission of Simon & Schuster, Inc. © 1956.

2. John Arthur Robinson, *Honest to God* (Philadelphia: Westminster Press, 1963).

Chapter 8

1. Calvin W. Taylor, *Creativity: Progress and Potential* (New York: McGraw-Hill, 1964), p. 179.
2. My thanks are due to John Cowan, my professional colleague, who helped develop the Creatrix to its present maturity.

Chapter 9

1. Irving L. Janis, "Groupthink," *Psychology Today,* November 1971, p. 43.
2. Jerry Harvey, "Managing Agreement in Organizations or: How to Cope with the Abilene Paradox." Unpublished manuscript, George Washington University Library, Washington, D.C., 1972.
3. William T. Sackett, Jr., Director, Research Department, Systems and Research Center. Honeywell interoffice correspondence 12 November 1971, "Organizational and Team Development and Groupthink."

Chapter 10

Chapter 10 is based on my article "How Much Risk Can You Afford to Take?" *Management Review,* May 1971, pp. 4–9.
1. Robert Townsend, *Up the Organization* (New York: Knopf, 1970), p. 115.

Chapter 12

Research in behavioral science literature for this chapter is summarized in R. E. Byrd, "Self Actualization Through Creative Risk Taking: A New Laboratory Model," unpublished Ph.D. thesis, New York University, 1970. For further information on various approaches to self-development, see David W. Johnson, ed., *Contemporary Social Psychology* (Philadelphia: Lippincott, 1973).
1. William C. Schutz, *FIRO-B Questionnaire* (Palo Alto, Calif.: Consulting Psychologist Press, 1967).
2. Gordon Allport, *Becoming* (New Haven, Conn.: Yale University Press, 1955), p. 66.

Chapter 13

1. David S. Brown, "The Professional Nurse Looks at Authority and Hierarchy," in Rachel Ayers, ed., *Looking Into Nursing Leader-*

ship (Washington, D.C.: Leadership Resources, Inc., 1966), p. 13. Reproduced by special written permission of the publisher.

2. For an excellent review of current practices in manpower planning, see Thomas H. Patten, *Manpower Planning and the Development of Human Resources* (New York: Wiley, 1971). Current marketing planning processes are well documented in Philip Kotler, *Marketing Management: Analysis Planning and Control,* 2nd edit. (Englewood Cliffs, N.J.: Prentice-Hall, 1972).

3. For an example of such a detailed planning program, see Paul E. Mott and Elsa A. Porter, "A Case Report on a Comprehensive Planning and Management System," *Action Research Papers Number 1* (Washington, D.C.: REB Associates, Inc., June 1973).

4. For one approach to wide involvement in setting objectives, see Richard E. Byrd and John Cowan, "MBO: A Behavioral Science Approach," *Personnel,* March-April 1974, pp. 42–50.

5. Frederick Herzberg, *Work and the Nature of Man* (New York: World Publishing, 1966).

6. Rensis Likert, *New Patterns of Management* (New York: McGraw-Hill, 1961).

7. Some 30 examples of corporate efforts to redesign work with greater self-direction given to employees are summarized in the appendix to *Work in America,* p. 188.

Chapter 14

1. J. W. Atkinson, ed., *Motives in Fantasy, Action, and Society* (Princeton, N.J.: Van Nostrand, 1958).

2. David C. McClelland, *The Achieving Society* (Princeton, N.J.: Van Nostrand, 1961).

3. H. H. W. Miles et al., "Psychosomatic Study of 46 Young Men with Coronary Artery Disease," *Psychosomatic Medicine,* Vol. 6, 1954, pp. 455–477. H. I. Russek, "Emotional Stress and Coronary Heart Disease in American Physicians, Dentists and Lawyers," *American Journal of Medical Science,* Vol. 243, 1962, pp. 716–726. R. Caplan, "Organizational Stress and Individual Strain: A Social-Psychological Study of Risk Factors in Coronary Heart Disease Among Administrators, Engineers and Scientists," Ph.D. dissertation, University of Michigan, 1971.

4. Sula Benet, "Why They Live to Be 100, or Even Older in Abkhasis," *The New York Times Magazine,* December 26, 1971.

5. George H. Litwin and Robert A. Stringer, Jr., *Motivation and Organizational Climate* (Boston: Harvard Business School, 1968).

6. For a fuller discussion of the program, see *Work in America,* pp. 85–95.

7. The only professional associations accrediting people in this field are the International Association of Applied Social Scientists, Inc., Washington, D.C., and the Association for Creative Change, Inc., Birmingham, Alabama. Others, uncertified except by experience or by good consulting firms, are also good. Pick your own, and pick carefully.
8. For a more detailed discussion, see Jack K. Fordyce and Raymond Weil, *Managing with People: A Manager's Handbook of Organization Development Methods* (Reading, Mass.: Addison-Wesley, 1971).

Chapter 15

A less complete version of this chapter appeared as "A Team Approach to Regaining Corporate Youth," *Management Review,* May 1973, pp. 9–18.
1. Thomas H. Patten, Jr., *Manpower Planning and the Development of Human Resources* (New York: Wiley, 1971), pp. 238–239.
2. Richard Beckhard, "The Confrontation Meeting," *Harvard Business Review,* Vol. 45, pp. 149–153.
3. Richard E. Byrd, "How Much Risk Can You Afford to Take?" *Management Review,* May 1971, pp. 4–9.
4. Warren G. Bennis and Philip E. Slater, *The Temporary Society* (New York: Harper & Row, 1968), pp. 104, 106.
5. Tom Alexander, "The Unexpected Payoff of Project Apollo," *Fortune,* July 1969, p. 114.
6. See Kay Harley, "Team Development," *Personnel Journal,* June 1971; and John H. Zenger and Dale E. Miller, "Building Effective Teams," *Personnel,* March-April 1974, pp. 20–29.
7. Goodwin Watson, "Resistance to Change," in Warren Bennis, Kenneth D. Benne, and Robert Chin, eds., *The Planning of Change* (New York: Holt, Rinehart and Winston, 1969), pp. 488–497.

Chapter 16

1. Rensis Likert, *New Patterns of Management* (New York: Mc-Graw-Hill, 1961).

Appendix

1. For example, *see* John E. Drotning, "Sensitivity Training: Some Critical Questions," *Personnel Journal,* November 1966, pp. 604–606; and Louis J. Schuster, "Needed: More Sensitivity, Less Training," *Personnel Journal,* August 1969, pp. 612–616.

2. Richard E. Byrd, "Redressing the Balance with Creative Risk Taking," *Adult Leadership,* November 1968, pp. 250–252. For information on another design variation, see Roger Harrison, "Developing Autonomy, Initiative and Risk Taking Through a Laboratory Design," paper presented at NTL Conference on New Technology in Organization Development, Washington, D.C., 1972.

3. ——, *Creative Risk Taking Training Laboratory: Book of Basic Readings,* 2nd edit. (Minneapolis, Minn.: Jones & Byrd, Inc., 1968).

4. The test is Everett L. Shostrom's *Personal Orientation Inventory* (San Diego, Calif.: Educational and Industrial Testing Service, 1962, 1963).

5. Gordon L. Lippitt, "Looking at Our Use of Time," *Training and Development Journal,* March 1969, p. 2.

6. Abraham Maslow, *Toward a Psychology of Being* (Princeton, N.J.: Van Nostrand, 1962), p. 191.

7. For details, see Richard E. Byrd, "Training in a Non-Group," *Journal of Humanistic Psychology,* Spring 1967, pp. 18–27.

8. Douglas Bunker, "The Effect of Laboratory Education Upon Individual Behavior," in Gerald G. Somers, ed., *Proceedings of the 16th Annual Meeting, Industrial Relations Research Association, December 1963* (Madison, Wis.: IRRA, 1964), pp. 220–232.

Index

absenteeism, women workers, 67

The Achieving Society (McClelland), 26, 31

achievement, fear of, 33–34

age and risk, 8

Agency for International Development, 184–185

alcohol and competence, 183–184

Alexander, Tom, 207

attitudes and team effectiveness, 55–56

authority
  and power, 132–134
  and risk, 13–14, 123–126
  sharing of, 78

Barrett, Michael R., on dilemma of middle manager, 4

Barry, A. G., 61

blacks as middle managers, obstacles facing, 65–66

board of directors, as environmental risk factor, 165

Boulle, Pierre, 43

The Bridge Over the River Kwai (Boulle), 43, 151

Brown, David, on forms of non-compliance, 170

candor vs. concealment in personal relationships, 79–81

Carnegie, Dale, 136

Cartwright, Dorwin, 49

challenge vs. threat, 20

challenger, as risk taker, 103–104

change
  need for, 7–9
  and risk, 8–9

client relationships as environmental risk factors, 166

climate, as organizational goal, 186–189

communication
  checklist, 178
  as organizational risk factor, 175–177

compensation
  of entrepreneurial team, 202–205
  of middle managers, 62–63

competence
  and corporate health, checklist of, 187
  defined, 181
  and deviousness or disrespect, 185–186
  and emotions, 185
  and managerial risks, 182
  and motivation orientation, 183
  and obsolescence, 184–185
  and optimism vs. cynicism, 182–183

243